4/9/11

To: Alice

May God bless you and
keep you always.

Vondalyn Shaw

When LEAVES FALL

Vondalyn Shaw

authorHOUSE®

AuthorHouse™
1663 Liberty Drive
Bloomington, IN 47403
www.authorhouse.com
Phone: 1-800-839-8640

First published by AuthorHouse 11/23/2010
ISBN: 978-1-4567-0154-3 (sc)
ISBN: 978-1-4567-0155-0 (e)

Library of Congress Control Number: 2010917336

Unless otherwise indicated, all Scripture quotations are from the New King James Version of the Bible.

Printed in the United States of America

This book is printed on acid-free paper.

Certain stock imagery © *Thinkstock.*

ANOINTED PUBLISHING HOUSE

Cover Design by:
Anointed Publishing House / 267-386-6361

Dedication

This book is dedicated to my loving and supportive husband Hakeem
Shaw and our beautiful and amazing sons Nasir and Samar.
I love you. I love you. I love you. xoxoxo

Thank you

Book Cover Design by   Anointed Publishing House

www.anointedpublishinghouse.com

Author's Photo by   Tyrone Love of Pixtions Photography

www.pixtions.com

Author's Hair by   Pietra Dunmore of Retrochic by Pietra

retrochicbypietra.com

Author's Makeup by   Lakisha Evans of Glorified Faces

www.GlorifiedFaces.com

(609) 284-5270

Acknowledgments

My beginning began with God so I'm beginning my acknowledgements with Him. Thank you Daddy for thinking me up. Thank You for my purpose. Thank you Lord Jesus for Your Holy Spirit. I'm so happy that 2010, is the year of Great Expectation for You! I want to make you proud.

I must acknowledge my husband Hakeem Shaw and our sons Nasir and Samar. Thank you for sharing me with our computer. Thank you for loving me and making each day worthwhile. I love you guys so very much!

To my mom Pearl Lee. Thank you for being a great role model. Thank you for taking Corey and I to church. It paid off and will continue to pay off. Thank you for your love and encouragement. Thank you for being my friend. Thank you for the stories you told me when I was little. Love you!

To my dad George Lee. Thank you for the good years and the years I look to in faith when you're a Believer.

To my brother Corey. When we all look back we'll smile and say "Thank God that's behind us." Love you.

To my Shaw family. Gilbert, Sylvia, and Khia. Thanks for your love, laughter, and support. Thanks for your dedication to family. Love you.

To my cousin J.L. Thank you for all the books I had access to growing up. Thank you for the time you spent with me. It really mattered. Thank you Joe for your wisdom. Love you guys.

To my cousin Kimesha Cooper. Keep it up girl! I'm looking forward to seeing the fruit of your labor.

To my Lee, Cooper, and Singletary family. God bless and let's keep the reunions going yall!

Thank you to my 4th grade English teacher Mrs. Barner (Shirley B. Foster Elementary), and my 11th grade English teacher Mrs. Patterson (Winslow High School). Mrs. Barner you were the very first person to tell me that my stories were interesting. You told me that you enjoyed reading my writing. I never forgot what you said. You also taught me the difference between dessert and desert. I still think about that short lesson whenever I write those words. Mrs. Patterson you were encouraging and motivating. Thank you for seeing something special in me. Thank you.

Thanks to my editor. Your encouragement, insight, and keen eye are what I needed. God Bless you.

Much thanks to Gwendolyn Ann Cook. Thank you for your loving and giving spirit. Thank you for your encouragement and the special prayers before we hang up from talking. You shared everything you had to give. Thank you so much and God Bless.

Last but not least, thank you to my Living Faith Christian Center family. Thank you Pastor Connie for your dedicated and loving leadership. Thank you for your guidance. And to Pastors Kevin Brown, Theodore Winsley, and Roosevelt Taylor, thank you for pouring into LFCC each time you speak.

Thank you to my G12 leader Brenda Henderson and my G12 sisters. I thank God for your smiling faces and hugs.

A special thanks to my endorsers for taking the time to read *When Leaves Fall* and for your positive feedback. You truly boosted my confidence.

Endorsements

"Praise God! This book really kept me on the edge of my seat. And as a new author Vondalyn's passion kept the storyline interesting from beginning to end. This is definitely a must read! Get yourself a cup of green tea, sit back, and allow yourself to be taken away as the leaves fall! I look forward to her next accomplishment."

- Gwendolyn Ann Cook, Believer/Author
"Women Walking in the Spirit Ministries" Founder

"Ms. Shaw has created a spiritual book that captures the essence of what we need to do in order that our dreams and visions can come true. We must embrace the power within. This power comes from the Creator. We also learn that our choices will direct our sustaining success. I am joyously anticipating her next book."

-Nicole Stephens, Ph.D.
Associate Professor of Education
Educational Specialist in Language, Reading, and Culture
Lincoln University of Pennsylvania

"Thought provoking and entertaining. *When Leaves Fall* is the best contemporary Christian novel I've read to date. Can't wait for the sequel."

- Danielle Henderson
Living Faith Christian Center
Pennsauken, NJ

"This book is one of those stories you want to go on forever. The book has constant action. It has so many riveting facets, including failures and successes of relationships in families and others. The characters were realistic. While children may be raised by the same parents, they take very different paths. The in-depth spiritual aspect was refreshing and showed the experiences that are had on the road of life with and without God's guidance. This story is great for book club reading."

- Gwen Knight
  Instructor of Business
  Camden County College
  C.H.I. Institute

"Wow!!! What an ending! I found the manuscript to be an easy read. I'm looking forward to the sequel."

- Marcella Edmunds
  Retired Sunoco Oil Corporate Employee

"*When Leaves Fall* is filled with colorful characters. It is a true page turner and a book with a moral lesson. Outstanding!"

- Jacqueline Jacobs-Lovell
  Ebenezer Baptist Church
  Englewood, NJ

Prologue

Just ahead are two images seemingly too bright to behold but you are not blinded. The sky is a familiar shade of blue though just a little more magnificent than you recall. The clouds are so bright and white that you reach out to touch them and believe that you actually can and you do.

There is singing all around and there are people all about- adults, children, and animals. You tune into the singing. It is everywhere- the sky, the grass, the flowers, the rocks, the trees. Everything and everyone is singing praises to God. Hallelujahs resound from every direction. You are in Heaven.

The two images are walking and talking. They turn to look intently at the other ever so often and gesture to each other. They smile and laugh. They both turn to smile back at you and you are overwhelmed with indescribable joy. You were already overflowing with happiness just being in the Kingdom. The bliss you feel is matchless. The two are the Father and Jesus. They have turned back around and began speaking again.

"Yes, our love can be resisted," said the Father, "but I will continue to reach out to them and they will reach back. Until then I long for them to stop trying to figure things out on their own. They use their gifts against the Kingdom and it saddens Me. James and Diane are My children. They will come to Me. Their families will call on Me in the midst of their trouble. I will answer them (Psalm 91:15).

In Jeremiah 29:11-14, God tells us that what He purposed for us to do, it shall be done. For He knows the thoughts He thinks toward us. They are not thoughts of evil, but good. He has a bright future planned for us. And when we call upon Him and go and pray to Him, He will listen to us. When we seek Him with our whole heart we will find Him and He will bring us out of whatever captivity we're in.

Chapter 1

Diane

"That's it. I'm leaving!"

January is very cold in the state of New Jersey! It's a blah type of month. It's the first month of the year, has thirty-one days, mostly gray skies, and no holidays besides New Year's Day which is of no importance to me because I've never gone out to celebrate it. And don't even talk about Martin Luther King, Jr. day. That's an important day! However, none of the bosses I've had seemed to think so.

Maneuvering my Volkswagen Beetle into one of the last parking spaces near Watson Hall, I shut off my car, put on my earmuffs, and gloves, pulled my hood over my head and ran to class only to discover that although I was running late, my professor hadn't shown up yet.

Tuning in and out of the different conversations around me I learned that my instructor only had fifteen more minutes before everyone could sign a makeshift attendance sheet and leave class. Just shy of two minutes before we could walk out Professor Timmons rushed into the classroom looking disheveled and straightening his tie as he almost crash-landed upon his usual perch on his desk. I rolled my eyes and bent to open my bag to pull out everything I needed for class.

Thirty minutes later I looked at the page in my notebook and stared at the date. I also glanced at the doodles I drew, then packed up to head for my next class. Just before I reached Thurston Hall, I decided to skip my other classes for that day and take off for who knows where. Back in my car I put the keys in the ignition to warm up but after seeing that my tank was almost below the empty line I tightened my hood and turned the key just enough so I could hear the radio.

At that moment the DJ announced that Corrina's latest song was about to come on and my heart danced because I knew all the words and felt I

1

could sing it just as well if not better than Corrina. My friends thought so too! I relished the thought of sitting somewhere and hearing my name and new song announced as people sat in their cars listening to my voice, my song. I imagined them grooving to my music on the dance floor.

When the song was over, I turned the key the rest of the way. I put the car in gear and drove off. No one but my friends and sister believed in my singing ability. They believed that I had the talent to become famous. My family couldn't deny my God given talent but they did not support me. I wanted them to support me when I entered talent shows or singing contests. They did not. It seemed like anything that had to do with singing and that made me happy my parents were against it. This made me feel miserable so because of that I wasn't totally free to be myself. I felt that my parents were trying to mold me into what they wanted me to be. My sister had dreams too! But she cared more about what our parents thought than pursing them.

My parents have been married twenty-five years. They have worked the same jobs forever with no motivation to get up and have something for themselves. My mother always talked about starting her own catering business. Whatever happened to that? – Nothing. That's what happened. She had all the resources she needed. She had the cooking ability, had the cooking tools she needed, and she had plenty of people from the neighborhood that would break their neck trying to get a plate of anything she cooked. But she never stepped out and did it.

At first when she talked about it when I was a little girl I marveled at the idea of helping her and my aunts and cousins set up pans of food to be taken to various places and eaten to celebrate weddings, funerals, birthdays, anniversaries, and holidays or whatever other occasions people get together for. But as my mother got older, every year I felt more sorry for her. I pitied her. I then became disappointed in her because I realized my mom was more satisfied with the idea of owning her own business than actually pursuing it.

My mom disappointed me because she constantly told me to never be afraid of anything. However, all I heard in my mother's voice was fear after her fantasizing was over because there was always a "but". And the "but" was always followed by a barrage of reasons why the catering business couldn't be pulled off. First of all it was never the right time because she wanted to wait for me and my sister Sharon to get a little older. Then she had to clear out space in the basement and probably the garage to store equipment. And of course she'd have to save up some money to buy a used car to make deliveries.

The list was endless. It became longer as the years passed. Her list of excuses was so long that when she began her fantasy catering business story I would get up and walk out of the room with some type of excuse so I wouldn't have to hear it. I believe in my mother because I know she's still able to live her dream. She's only fifty-six, with plenty of good years ahead of her. The only thing holding her back is fear.

Then there's daddy. At sixty, he's still capable of obtaining his dream. Of all the memories, I have of my dad my mind is flooded with mental pictures of him carrying bags of grass seed, fertilizer, flowers, and yard tools. Whenever I heard the "beep-beep" of Larry's Landscaping truck I ran out the house to help dad pile up the wheelbarrow with the mulch that was dumped in the yard. I loved the deep black color of the mulch and the moist coolness of it in my hands. Many times, I was tempted to lay face down in it to feel it on my face. But I stopped just shy of doing it because of the smell.

My dad knew everything about gardening, maintaining the lawn, growing things, killing weeds and grass, and creating beautiful landscape designs with bushes, flowers, plants, stones, and wood. I used to smile at him when he walked across the street to stand at the edge of the Floyd's yard to get a better view of what he created. He'd take his straw hat off, wipe his bald head and forehead with a handkerchief then replace his hat. Then he'd take a stance with his legs spread just so and cross his arms across his strong broad chest and silently approve of his work proudly with a nod of his head.

Sometimes from my hiding place, I saw him look down as if in thought but not of pleasant thoughts but thoughts of what if or of things not obtained or to never be obtained. Those were the times I'd pull out my secret weapon to brighten those sad eyes. I'd go to my little corner in the shed in the back yard and pull out my small spray bottle of miracle grass, weed, plant, ant, bug, and worm destroyer. It was a mixture of WD-40, gasoline for the lawnmower container, liquid detergent, and fabric softener and whatever else I deemed worthy to be included in it. I'd shake it up and commence to spraying, then I'd run to meet daddy as he was walking across the yard and grab his big, powerful hand and lead him to my latest victim.

One particular time, I managed to kill some type of bug that was resting on a weed as well as the weed itself in one day. I was rather proud of what I'd accomplished because my previous experiments required me to spray things a few times over a couple of days before something actually died. Well, the insects always died but those stubborn weeds were hard to beat. Daddy always knelt down on his haunches balancing me on his knees. He'd tell me that I really gave it to that weed or bug then he'd smile and pinch my cheek and tell me that he was proud of me. Then the sadness in his eyes would leave because he was thinking of me. I think he was thinking of the hope he had in me. I don't know.

Mom's worst enemy was herself and her lack of confidence in her ability to try something new. Dad's problem was his so called friends. I know this because one day I was eavesdropping on a conversation dad was having with two men from the neighborhood that would come by and sit and talk with him while he was changing the oil on the car or tinkering in the garage. Occasionally they'd go fishing or help dad with yard work. Well, on this day I was sitting on the floor in the room right next to the garage playing jacks. I heard a car pull into the driveway so I jumped to peek out the window. It was Mr. Brandon and Mr. Sonny.

Usually Mr. Sonny walked to the house but not that day. I suspected that as Mr. Brandon was on his way he stopped to pick up Mr. Sonny as a favor, explaining why the two of them showed up together. One door slammed then another, then I heard footsteps come into the garage and stop right in front of the door I was leaning against listening through. I heard dad greet them and offer them something to drink, but neither wanted anything because they wouldn't be staying long.

Mr. Brandon asked dad what he was doing and dad explained that he was writing down a list of the products he intended to buy in order to jump start his landscaping business. Both Mr. Brandon and Mr. Sonny started saying things like daddy should take a little more time to think about taking such a big step and was he sure about it and what did my mom think and how he expected to make it if he didn't get all the customers he hoped to get.

Dad said he thought about all that but he'd have to take that chance. Mr. Brandon laughed and said daddy was a fool to think that he could become successful at this and that he didn't even have any help and what would happen during the winter when people wouldn't need his services. But daddy didn't say anything. I expected him to respond in some way but he didn't. I just heard him open a cabinet and put something in it. Then he closed it. I heard the folding chairs around the little table scrape across the floor and then someone shuffling cards. Usually I was excited when dad and his friends played cards because they got loud and laughed and cracked jokes, and told stories from when they were younger and had good times. Sometimes daddy let me sit on his knee to teach me how to play by telling me what card to throw out.

I loved those times. But this time I stayed inside because the conversation wasn't the same. Instead of talking about back in the day they were talking about the days ahead and putting daddy down because he had a dream. Neither one of them had any hopes and dreams except to stay the same way never reaching and striving for anything because they had a poverty mentality. Daddy didn't see it. He didn't know how to recognize it. He didn't even realize that they were jealous of him. Yes they were envious! He just did not realize it. One day I overheard Mr. Brandon and Mr. Sonny ask if daddy had come to his senses. Daddy offered them a seat and pulled out the deck of cards never to open that notebook that contained an alternate future again.

After they left I walked into the garage. Daddy was folding up the chairs and putting them on the wall onto nails he hammered to hold them. I gathered all the playing cards and chips and put them away. We moved around in silence until my little girl mind came up with the idea to tell daddy that he didn't have to worry about help because Sharon and I could help. I said even though Sharon was busy with music, boys, and kissing and stuff that I could talk her into helping. We'd work on everyone's yard in the neighborhood, then the whole city, then the state.

I knew that wasn't possible but I had so much faith in dad. I knew he could do anything. He was my hero. Mr. Brandon and Mr. Sonny were becoming like kryptonite to my Superman and I couldn't stand it. Daddy came over to me for what I thought was going to be a great big thank you and a pinch on the cheek, but instead he bent down on his haunches so he was at my level and held my face in his hands. He looked at me for what seemed like an eternity and I saw myself in his eyes. His face didn't show happiness, anger, or anything- but yes it did. It showed sorrow. Sorrow in the fact that he wasn't who I believed him to be.

He didn't say anything. But his face spoke volumes, then he said, "Diane, you're too young. You haven't lived long enough to understand that you're going to be unhappy most days. Honey, you just don't understand the world. Your belief in "happily ever after" only exists in your little story books."

But my belief wasn't in the world. It was in my father. I had parents who were lost in the idea of their dreams instead of the pursuit of them

I was raised in an environment of failure. I heard somewhere that we're products of our environment. I don't know that that's totally true. People seem to think that the apple never falls far from the tree, or that we're chips off the old block as my dad used to say. I beg to differ. What about those who come from good, supportive families that end up going nowhere in life? Or what about those with parents that are druggies or alcoholics that become doctors or lawyers or succeed in some other field?

I think that our environment plays an important role. But I believe that what's inside of us plays an even bigger role. You can see wrong and decide you're going to be right. Or you can see nothing and become nothing. My parents certainly aren't nothing because they're hardworking people filled with a lot of love. They met in the south and were both children of parents who could barely make ends meet. Both my grandfathers were sharecroppers and both my grandmothers cleaned and cooked for whites as well as blacks. Both of their families were large. They produced at least eight to ten kids a piece. I think the more people are told that they'll never be anything they begin to believe it.

Once that seed is sown and takes root, it guides their thoughts and actions. They have a poverty mentality. They pass that cursed way of living and decision making on to their children. I believe they mean well by not wanting their children to take chances and risk losing everything they have, but what is life without chances and risks?

ʕ϶

Sitting at the gas station waiting for the attendant to take the hose out and close my tank I made the decision to change my major. It's a decision I felt totally confident about within the safety of my beetle but once I sit in front of my parents to tell them I'm changing my major to music I'll feel like jelly.

Throwing down my bag on the family room sofa I thought about my sister Sharon who recently graduated from college with a degree that my parents approved of which helped her to get a boring position at some company in a city we've never heard of, so she can work a predictable nine-to-five day and have a predictable hum-drum life. Sharon is a natural-born dancer. She has great talent. Whatever moves we saw on television she only needed to see once and she'd do the same thing as if in instant replay mode and add a little extra just because she wanted to show off. She would tell me whether or not she dug the moves and if she didn't she'd tell me what she would've and would not have done.

Her face glowed when she danced. I loved watching her groove to the flow of the music. She tried unsuccessfully to teach me all the latest moves. All I was able to master was The Bump. I can't dance and Sharon can't sing but the two of us together were something magical. When Sharon told me that she contacted a school of dance out of state she said there was no way mom and dad could say no. She had everything planned out and rehearsed. She had props and everything. She was so happy, but although mom and dad sat through her presentation they said no.

They came up with all kinds of reasons why she shouldn't do it, then why she couldn't do it. I refused to sit facing her like mom and dad because I didn't want to see her face deflate. Just before she turned to go to her bedroom after packing up her props, she said that she was going to be a dancer no matter what they said. Mom and dad responded that not one cent of their money was going to pay for her to go to some dance school to be dancing around like a fool with no clothes on her back and no roof over her head. Sharon's eyes filled with tears and she ran to her room. I never saw her dance again. At least not like she used to. There was no soul in it – no life nor passion. She was just going through the motions. I was not looking forward to this, but I had to let them know how I felt. I was prepared for them to shoot me down like they did Sharon but not for what happened next.

"Mom, dad, I have something very important to talk to you guys about," I said. I saw my mom looking at me sideways as she and my dad sat down at the kitchen table.

"No, I'm not pregnant," I said, knowing my mom's thoughts. I saw and heard her release a breath of relief as she cut herself a slice of chocolate cake and placed it on a napkin.

"Ok, so what is it then?" She asked in a get it over with already tone.

"Well," I said, "my second semester started not too long ago and I've decided to change my major like we talked about if I didn't like my classes."

"Alright, we're listening," my mom said.

My heart beating quicker and my blood thumping in my ears, I felt my legs begin to shake with nervousness.

"I don't know why I'm afraid," I said to myself. *"They're my parents and they love me. I love them."* But then I remembered how their love ended Sharon's dreams of being a dancer. I decided to get it over with.

"I hate my classes at Vernard Community College, I knew I'd never like it and I never wanted to go in the first place. I don't want to be a nurse. I want to sing for a living. But if I can at least change my major so I can study music then I'll be satisfied for now but at least it's better than studying something I could care less about regardless how great the demand for nurses is. I'm prepared to change my major to music at the end of this semester in May," I shot out like an auctioneer. I saw the disappointment come over their faces and I knew things weren't going to be easy.

"Diane I'm surprised you're just coming to us about this," my dad said.

"Quite frankly, I thought you would've tried to start buttering us up before you graduated from high school," my mother said.

"But I didn't because I knew what you would say and I was hoping that after some time passed you'd change your mind," I said close to pleading.

"Well, just so you know you would've gotten the same answer you're getting today," my dad responded sternly. "The answer is no," he said, "And I don't want to hear another thing about it. Case closed," he almost yelled as he slammed his fist on the table with the last two words.

I was a little hurt because my dad had never showed any anger toward me– ever.

"Diane, your dad and I didn't work hard raising you girls to grow up and sing and dance in clubs. That just doesn't make any sense to me," my mom said.

"We're not talking about Sharon and me. We are talking about me and my life," I said staring bullets out the kitchen window to make sure I didn't dare challenge either of them. It was becoming hard to do, but I was keeping my cool.

"I'm sick and tired of hearing you talk about singing and music and performing and records. Singing isn't a practical or reliable profession and quite frankly there's no real chance that you'll ever make it big so to ensure that there are no disappointments, you better forget about this and either stick with nursing or maybe become a teacher," she said popping her neck and pointing her finger at me.

"Ok, I can major in music and minor in teaching and maybe in between pursue my music career," I said.

"Ok, bottom line is we don't approve of you singing, scattin' or doing anything else associated with music because we don't want you to get your hopes up and end up being disappointed," my dad said.

After that I'd had it and my pulse was racing.

"You don't want me to pursue my dreams! This is my life!" I yelled at the top of my voice. My mom gave me a "you better act like you know" look that would've worked had I been my old self. I put my hand on my hip and started moving my neck around.

"All you want to do is stifle my dreams so I won't have a future like the two of you! You want me to walk around scared lacking confidence in myself and caring more about what people think than what I know about me!" I screamed. "You guys never became anything more than what you started out as but you had dreams. What happened? Mom you used to talk about a catering business all the time and dad you used to talk about doing your own landscaping thing. You two are just two old scared black people that don't have nothin', don't want nothin', and aint ever gonna have nothin' because you're scared of failing! Well, you've already succeeded at that because you've failed me by not going after a better life for yourselves and our family," I said quieting down. "Don't you want me to have more than you have in life? Don't you want the next generation to be extraordinary?"

After no response I stood there and screamed as loud as I could until my mom got up and slapped the taste out of my mouth. My cheek and eye stinging, I put my hand to my watering eye and said, "I hate you. I hate both of you," and turned to go to my room.

"Don't you walk away from us!" my mother yelled.

But I kept on walking. The next thing I knew my head snapped back because my mom grabbed a handful of my hair and tried to pull me down onto my back.

"Mary, stop it!" my dad yelled as he pulled us apart.

"What's going on here?" he questioned in a frenzy. "Is this how we act now? Do we start yelling and screaming and fighting now when we don't get our way? Now Diane, you were wrong because you were very disrespectful to your mother and I and you better apologize right now!" he ordered.

"You better apologize right now!" my mom yelled.

My face was still stinging and the back of my head was pounding. I bent down to pick up some of my hair from the floor and cursed under my breath.

"You don't mean that Mary," my dad said, "Just let things cool down a bit and let's talk a little later," he said calmly.

Not wanting the fiasco to continue, I mumbled that I was sorry and my mom looked at me. She apologized, as well. As I was turning to go upstairs, I saw her holding out her arms for a hug, but I continued toward the steps as if I hadn't noticed. That day caused me to go beyond a limit I never imagined venturing into, but I went there that day.

I closed my bedroom door and sat on my bed holding my head with all kinds of wild thoughts going through my mind. I felt like I couldn't live if I wasn't living my dream. I couldn't live if I wasn't living my dream. I'd saved up $3,000.00 which included birthday money, money for this and that and money from part time jobs I had over the past two years and money I earned helping my dad in the yard, plus money I received from family for graduation. Sitting in my room I made a decision that would change my life forever.

I decided to take the money I had and leave home. I was going to live my life with no regrets. I had to see if I had what it takes to make it. If I didn't believe in myself who would? I thought about calling Sharon to visit her for a while until I figured out what to do next but she would have eventually folded under the pressure of my parent's constant badgering. I couldn't tell my friends either. I wanted to be able to tell my parents that I was leaving but that wouldn't work out. Instead of leaving without a word I decided to leave a letter explaining why I was leaving. I really did have good parents except for their lack of support.

The next day started like an ordinary day for me except for me packing everything I could into my car after my parents left for their respective jobs. I left the letter on my parent's bed. I walked back to my room taking a final look and I was gone. Not knowing where I was going excited me and scared me to death. It was almost as if I was afraid of making my own decisions despite the need to make my own decisions being the reason I was leaving.

Driving down Fourth Avenue, I paid unusual attention to the houses I drove past everyday. A few minutes later I approached Claudette's house. Claudette was my "homegirl". Seeing that she must've been running late for class I almost turned into her driveway to tell her what I was doing and ask her to say a prayer of safety for me, but I kept going.

Listening to the radio, I learned there was a singing contest scheduled in two weeks and the winner would be given the chance to audition with Trevor and his band. The DJ said that's how Trevor got his start and he was the biggest thing out these days. I got a familiar feeling of anticipation, nervousness, excitement, and uncertainty in my stomach when the announcer said the contest was in Los Angeles.

I'd never been to L.A. and thought about turning around and going home but I couldn't because I kept seeing my parents and hearing the things I said to them ring in my ear. I had to prove something to them. I had to prove something to myself. The furthest I'd ever driven was to Rhode Island to visit family. The ride was about five hours but two of my cousins were with me. This time I'd be by myself. I wished I had someone with me.

I grabbed a map of the U.S. from a gas station and mapped out my journey. Leaving New Jersey wasn't hard to do. I'd been there for eighteen years and had only visited a few other states all of which were on the east coast. Besides, my future awaited me.

Chapter 2

James

He gave me new life!

I love winter. Though I didn't always love it. When I was a kid I liked springtime and summer. Spring meant the weather breaking and baseball season and summer meant no school, long days, swimming, and hanging out with friends. Good times. Then life began to happen. I was about fifteen when Pop got sick. I noticed little things here and there like his gradual weight loss and the fact that he miraculously quit smoking cigarettes.

I remember when Ma used to smoke too. However after going to church with one of her friends from work she decided to quit. I remember it being hard at first and sometimes she cried. Then one day as I was on my way to my room I heard her talking and mumbling in her bedroom so I peeked in and saw her on her knees leaning on the bed praying. There were many more times I saw and heard her praying and I even caught her smoking a cigarette here and there but after several months passed she and her clothes didn't have the familiar cigarette scent.

Mom seemed happier and livelier. She had overcome something. I asked her once why she started smoking in the first place. She said there were a lot of reasons. But the main one was that her best friend in high school started smoking after taking some from her brother's stash in his room. The next thing she knew one cigarette here and there became one cigarette a day, then two, then after each time she ate, then one as soon as she woke up, then one right after work until she was smoking a pack a day.

When she met dad, he didn't smoke or drink or anything. At first he was turned off when he saw her smoking and said it wasn't something a lady should do. She said that if he really liked her he had to accept her the way she was – take her or leave her. And he did. He took her. Mom used to get up and do what she called sashaying and say dad couldn't resist her. My little sister Erica would get up and try to copy her. I told her she was strong and she used to say that she never would've been able to kick the habit if it weren't for Jesus.

She told me that Jesus obediently allowed Himself to be sacrificed in our place so that we could be free from bondage like her addiction to cigarettes, sin, any sickness or disease, and anything else you could imagine. Whenever I told her that something was hard or difficult for me in school or whatever I was going through, no matter what it was she'd always tell me that "I could do all things though Christ who strengthens me."

My mom quit smoking when I was fourteen. My dad started getting sick sometime that next year. Once, my mom told me in a moment of weakness that she felt guilty and responsible for my dad getting sick because she gave him his first cigarette and he ended up developing a greater habit than she did. She started to cry. I pulled her to me and hugged her while telling her that she didn't make him smoke it. It was his decision. At that moment, I felt a great heaviness weigh on me in the center of my chest. At that time our roles changed and I was no longer her son but her protector and it scared me because I knew that it very well might become my reality.

I started going to church with my mom and sister not long after feeling the heaviness. I didn't know why but I didn't notice the weight so much when I was there. One Sunday the pastor spoke on making the right decisions and allowing the Holy Spirit to be a part of every area of your life. Then just like every other service one of the ministers announced offering and afterward he did the altar call.

There was nothing special or out of the ordinary about that day, but when the musicians began to play softly and the choir matched them by singing just as soft I felt different. The minister asked if there were any in the church that had made wrong decisions and people raised their hand, including my mom and little sister. He talked a bit more summarizing the sermon then asked if there was anyone that wanted to be saved. Those words shocked me somehow. Not my mind but my body.

It seemed like the heaviness in my chest spread and I felt heavy all over. My head began to pound as the minister said almost the same words he said every Sunday inviting people to get saved. With every word my head pounded harder and harder as if something heavy was on me and I began to sweat. My heart pounded because I realized that I was thinking I should get up and stand in the line to get saved.

I was going through something on that seat but didn't know what. I looked around and I saw others looking around although the minister said everyone should be praying with their eyes closed. Reasons why I shouldn't get up were filling my mind. *What would the people in the church think of me and what would the girls think that I noticed checking me out since I'd been going to their church? I couldn't get up there and make a fool of myself. What if I got up and stepped on someone's foot? It was going to be too much trouble for me to walk by everyone to get in the prayer line. I could do it another day when not as many people were there.* When the minister spoke it was as if he were reading my mind.

"The devil will try to talk you out of getting saved by making you think of all kinds of excuses. Please don't leave here today without giving your life to Christ because you don't know if today is the last day of your life."

That really got to me. I couldn't imagine what it would be like to die because I wanted to live and living was all I knew how to do. Death was far beyond my thinking ability. Then the minister spoke again.

"I know many of you are thinking that you'll do it next Sunday or during midweek service, but what if there's no next time for you?"

The next thing I knew I was standing up. I started walking toward the end of the pew crossing over the people I didn't want to cross over and walking by the girls that had been watching me and I hoped to date one day. Although the walk to the end of the prayer line wasn't long it seemed like it was a mile. I continued to sweat and my legs shook but I kept on walking.

My head, ears, and heart were still pounding. But my mind gave me the most trouble. It was still fighting me and telling me to make up another reason for getting in line like wanting prayer but not to get saved. I felt everyone was watching me and I wondered what they were thinking. They probably thought my mom made me get in line or something. I thought about the mental battle I was going through and how when I was sitting down, in my mind I kept hearing something say *"get in line, go get in line"* and I kept thinking *"no, no, no."*

About ten people were in line ahead of me and some were teenagers like me. I wondered if everyone in line experienced the same thing I did in order to get up. I tried to focus on the back of the head of the woman ahead of me. Her hair smelled like it had been hot-combed. I knew this because every Saturday night my mom pressed her and Erica's hair so it would be straight for Sunday. Her hair smelled like some kind of grease. I noticed that she or whoever she had pressing her hair branded her on the back of her neck.

The line moved. It moved a little more until I was next. A couple of the people in line ahead of me fell out and fell backward which made me take a step back as everyone ahead of me took a step back to keep from getting stepped on. The men and women in charge of catching the people weren't doing a good job that day and I desperately hoped I wouldn't fall back because I'd never come back to church again. I'd definitely have no chance with any of those girls that I imagined laughing at me and the guys I played ball with every now and then would probably think I was a punk.

It was my turn.

The pastor was standing directly in front of me while two ministers stood behind him on either side praying. On either side of me was an elder but one of them had a little brown bottle from the drugstore made for cough syrup in his hand that had some kind of oil in it. He tilted the bottle back once then painted a cross on my forehead. Then they began to pray as the pastor gripped my forehead pushing me back. I used the muscles in my neck to keep myself standing straight.

"Son, did you come up to be saved?" he asked.

"Yes Sir."

"Son, this is the most important decision you'll ever make in your life. Raise your hands and repeat after me."

I had to renounce Satan and believe that God loved the world so much that He sent His son Jesus to die on the cross for me. He said Jesus took all my sins upon Himself willingly and allowed Himself to be punished in my place and died. Lastly I had to believe that Jesus rose from the dead three days later defeating death and sin. All I had to do was repeat what he said, believe it, and I was saved. And I did.

I felt an overwhelming urge to cry just before my prayer was complete. I feared I couldn't control it. I couldn't because the tears came. I'd never cried in public but I'd seen men cry in church since I'd been attending so I found some comfort in that as the pastor hugged me and sent me on my way.

Walking to my seat I dried my eyes with my sleeve and felt oil running down my forehead between my eyes on its way to the bridge of my nose. As I stepped over everyone on the way to my seat I saw that my mom had been crying and she smiled then mouthed, *"Thank you Jesus"* and raised her hands. I finally sat down and she turned and hugged me real quick. I felt a few pats on my back and my shoulders from various people and I felt drained. I felt like what it must feel like to climb a mountain, but I felt peaceful inside. Even though I didn't want to, I needed to cry because it felt right. I felt new.

On the way home and even once we got home my mom never said anything to me about what happened at church. I know it was because she thought I would get mad about her talking about me crying and then hugging me and stuff. She's right though. But I saw her smiling at me from time to time. Then one day I guess she couldn't take it anymore and left a letter on my bed telling me how proud she was of me. I held on to that letter for years.

In the meantime my dad had good days and bad days dealing with the pancreatic cancer that was eating him alive. During that first and second year dad could work but he slowed down considerably. Everyone kept telling him to take it easy but he was determined to support his family like a man. I remember how he often talked to me about being a man and what it took to be a man. He told me that being able to make babies didn't make me a man because anything with a penis can make a baby, if given the opportunity.

He gave me a knowing look and I knew what it meant. He told me what to look for in a wife and a lot of other things about women. Dad shared a lot with me those last three years of his life. He also shared with me that he'd put $10,000 away that my mom didn't know about. So when he died mom would get $250,000 and my sister and I both would get $100,000 each.

I didn't want to hear anything about him dying but our talk was necessary. He told me where to find all the necessary paperwork for the insurance policies. He trusted me with the information he gave me. He wanted me to take care of my mom and sister. I had to promise that I wouldn't let our family go broke and that I wouldn't let him down.

He held me at arms length by the shoulders and looked at me. I'll never forget what he said next, "I love you son," then he hugged me and I turned to leave the room. Just before I got to the door I heard his voice again and I turned around to hear him say, "Real men serve God and I'm very proud of you."

With that he shook out the newspaper next to him and started reading again. I walked off feeling good that my dad trusted me because growing up I'd done some things that my parents were less than pleased about. I was glad that I'd regained his trust and that he trusted me with his wife and daughter.

Then the day came that I became the man of the house. We all knew that day was coming soon and we had all pretty much accepted that any day there would be three of us. Dad had been making rattling and gurgling sounds in his throat, throughout the morning and he had suffered long enough. Deep down when it was my turn to check on him, I wished and prayed that he'd already be gone. Mom called our pastor over and she, Erica, and I sat on the bed in my parent's room holding hands and each touching dad.

In my mind, he was still the strong man I knew just a few years ago, and I pressed hard to be. But when I opened my eyes he looked like a wooden skeleton because he hardly had any meat or muscle on his body. His eyes and cheeks were sunken and on more than one occasion I woke up in a sweat after dreaming of him. Pastor said he wanted to pray for dad and asked if he wanted to pray the prayer of salvation again. When he said "again" I looked at mom and she shook her head yes.

The burden I carried that my dad would spend eternity in hell lifted. Then I watched as tears continued to drop one by one from mom's red and swollen eyes. Erica sat silently with tears gathered under her chin. However, I could tell she wouldn't be able to hold it in much longer.

We all prayed along with pastor and dad, then a tear left dad's left eye as he looked at each of us. He was so weak and so frail. He didn't say a lot, but it seemed like so much time had passed until he finished because of his labored breathing.

"I love the three of you so much. I want you to be strong. You have to be strong for each other. James, remember what I told you. Baby," he said slowly turning to look at my mom, "I have always and will always love you and I'll be waiting for you." My mom broke down right then and laid over him crying loudly. My sister had let go then too after dad called her his little girl and told her other things that were special to only the two of them.

We all lay on dad when he finished speaking and I felt the skeleton of his frame and began to cry. We laid there until Pastor touched my back softly and said, "He's gone son. He's gone on to be with the Lord. What you all are laying on is just a shell. His spirit is with God."

I sat up and touched my mom. She already knew. I got up and walked out the room walked through the house, walked out the door and got into my car.

Dad prepared us for this. We missed him. We cried. But we moved on. By this time, I'd already graduated high school and from the local junior college majoring in business. By the time I graduated Erica was sixteen and had begun dating dudes I didn't approve of and I let them know it. She didn't speak to me for a while but eventually she met another guy who had some things going for himself so I gave my approval for them to date.

Mom met a man at the grocery store about eight months after dad died and they seemed to hit it off. After the funeral, I thought about the possibility that someone may step up and show interest in her, but I didn't know how I'd feel about that until it actually happened. Mom never said anything to me and I later found out that she didn't say anything to Erica either. I truly believe that was the best way for her to let us know that she was ready to move on with her life. If presented with a situation and given the chance to express your opinion you don't always respond in the way the other person hopes. I'm glad she didn't ask me at the time because I probably would've been angry.

I loved seeing my mom get all dressed up, getting her hair done, and wearing makeup again. It made me feel good inside. I knew I didn't have to worry about her adjusting to life with dad gone. Erica wasn't a little girl anymore so between her girlfriends and the guy she was seeing I hardly ever saw her. It seemed like everyone was moving on except me. It's not that I was still grieving but I had no plans. I didn't know what I wanted to do with my life at the moment. What I did know is that I wanted to finish my degree in business but I also wanted to travel. I'd only been to a few states outside of Jersey like Maryland, Delaware, North and South Carolina but I wanted to see more.

One night, about a year after dad died mom and the guy she'd been seeing came home early and announced they were getting married. I had been feeling a little guilty for wanting to leave home but I realized mom and Erica didn't need me as much as I thought- which was cool. Not long after they were married, I packed up and told everyone I was leaving. Mom and Erica were sad to see me go and my new step dad John took me to the side to make sure that it wasn't because of him. I assured him that wasn't it and after telling him why I needed to leave home he totally understood where I was coming from. We shook hands and I was off.

A week or two before, I bought a brand new Chevy truck with some of the money I received after dad's passing. It was a truck I had my eye on ever since it first came out but I definitely couldn't afford it. I beat myself up a little because the only reason I could afford the truck was because dad died and I wondered if I should've bought something used instead. With mom and John's encouragement they helped me to see that dad was smiling down at me and encouraging me to be the best I could be. They said dad was happy that he was able to leave something behind to help me. I knew deep down they were right so I got over the guilt.

My truck was packed, I had a full tank of gas, and a cooler full of sandwiches, sodas, and snacks that mom made. As I drove along I thought about the places I wanted to go. I couldn't decide which direction to take – north, south, or west. I decided to go west because there was more to see. It was just me and God in that truck and I talked out loud to Him, and for the first time ever I heard Him speak to me.

It had been just a month since I had been filled with the Holy Spirit. I had also been going to Wednesday night church services ever since. I was learning a lot and praying more. I even started taking notes like I was in class. I didn't want to leave my church nor the friends I made and even more, Danielle. Danielle was special to me and turned out to be one of the girls that was checking me out the day I got saved. She walked up to me after Wednesday night service a couple weeks after and commented on my response to a question that was posed in a brief conversation I was having with another girl.

I could tell she liked me. I believe that she knew I was interested in her too. A few days later I called her and asked her out. I took her to dinner and a movie. I liked Danielle because she's cool. She wasn't like other girls I dated in high school and college. They weren't about anything. Someone like Danielle I'd be willing to wait for. I don't know why – well, maybe I do, but I found myself taking her out less and she stopped calling me as much. When we saw each other at church we'd speak and sometimes hug, then that stopped too.

I guess I pushed her away when I told her I had no plans to get married anytime soon. I knew from our first date that she definitely was the type that a man would settle down with and marry, but not now. She said she wasn't interested in dating just to date because she was looking for a husband. I suppose we pushed each other away. So with no loose ends I left Jersey in peace as I headed west to California.

CHAPTER 3

Diane

Out with the old... In with the new...

It took me about a week to drive to California. It was an awesome experience driving across the country by myself with my own thoughts and fantasizing about my future. In the back of my mind I wondered how I was going to make it on my own in a state I knew nothing about and didn't know anyone. Something I've always found interesting when traveling across states is how radio stations change. I don't even remember how many times I had to change the station to find a good R&B song.

The talent show was still on for the upcoming week and I had so much to do before I could even concentrate on it. First of all, I didn't know my way around the city and I'd heard so much about gangs, gang colors, and territory wars that I didn't know whether what I had on was safe to wear. Seeing a newspaper stand up ahead I pulled over to buy a paper and a snack to eat. Sitting in my car I munched on a bag of chips and a Dr. Pepper scanning the local paper to see if I could learn a little something about the city I now called home.

Leaving Jersey and its thirty degree and below temperatures in January was easy to do especially since it was over sixty degrees in L.A. After reading about some local news, I flipped through to the classified section and found some information that would help me get started. There was a boarding house located in a suburb of L.A. called Burbank. I remembered seeing a sign for Burbank not too far back. The boarding house had rooms for rent at $20.00 a week. Rent included three meals a day, linens, and a wreck room. I circled the ad and kept looking.

I knew $3,000 was enough to last me for a while but I had enough sense to know that I better secure a job now rather than later. I found two openings but neither of them was anything that jumped out and grabbed

20

my attention. One opening was for a waitress at a diner and the other position was for a legal assistant at a law firm.

Peeking in my side mirror to check for traffic I got out of my car and walked to a payphone to call the boarding house. Thankfully there were two rooms left and if I hurried I could get the larger of the two. When I got back in the car I quickly jotted down the directions. According to the woman I spoke with I wasn't far from the boarding house.

When I was a few blocks away from my new home I stopped at a corner store called Manny's. There were men standing in front of the entrance and I was nervous. I didn't know whether they were going to say something to me or not let me inside the store. As I lifted my foot to the first step one of the guys put his foot in my way. I stopped in my tracks. I took a deep, nervous breath and looked him in the eye. He stared at me for a second then dismissed me when he pulled his foot away and took a bottle in a paper bag from his pocket and started to drink.

Once inside I grabbed a few things I needed then looked through the freezer for an ice cream sandwich. I noticed who I guessed to be Manny behind the counter on the phone. He wasn't trying to hide the fact that he was watching my every move, and I figured since he didn't know me he was making sure I didn't steal from him. When I reached the counter I laid everything down one by one and estimated the total bill. I loved guessing how much cashiers would say. If I got it right I imagined I won a million dollars. If I came close I'd still win something.

The man I figured to be Manny asked me if I found everything okay and I told him I did. My total was $31.54. Shoot, I guessed $32.00. Oh, well, I still win. I rummaged through my purse then pulled out two twenties. Making sure I had my directions straight I asked if he knew of the boarding house I was going to and he did. He told me to go up two more blocks and make a left. The house I was looking for would be on the right hand side about four or five houses down. I thanked him and walked out, brushing by Manny's guard dogs then getting into my car and locking the doors.

When I stopped in front of the house I turned the car off and pulled up the emergency brake because the street was a slight hill. The street was nice and clean with trees up and down both sides that cascaded over the street creating a shady look as you drove along. All the homes were well taken care of and had neatly manicured yards. The home I hoped to live in was two stories. It had a porch that almost wrapped around the whole house.

There was a set of stairs that lead to a porch on the upper level of the house and there were three doors labeled "A, B, and C" that each had their own mail slot. I began to get excited with the thought of having my own space and being on my own. There were six wide cement steps with a railing on each side that led to the enormous front porch. When I got out the car I was then able to truly take in the magnificence of the house. It was white with black shutters with white steps and iron rails painted black.

The front porch above and on the main level were painted black and the roof was a dark grey. The house was beautiful. For me, it was the most stunning home on the street. There were bushes and flowers planted all around the house in different colors. Some were red, white, and yellow and were planted in multi-colored bunches. On both sides of the house there were lemon and avocado trees. Approaching the house, I took a deep breath in anticipation and walked up the sidewalk, up the steps, across the porch, and into the house.

Meticulously shined dark wooden floors were everywhere. There were paintings on just about every wall and a long staircase that lead upstairs. Although the yard left a lasting impression the inside of the house seemed like another world. I'd never been in anything so immaculate before. As I walked deeper into the home, I noticed some carpeted rooms like the recreation room that had a pool table, ping pong table, stereo, and a television in it. Two comfortable looking couches were placed in one area along with a few cushioned sitting chairs.

People were relaxing in this room playing pool or watching television. Across the hall was another carpeted room that was a little more laid back with people watching television with the volume down real low and playing board games. Right next to that room was a quiet room where people lounged reading magazines, books, and the newspaper and the walls were covered from end to end and ceiling to floor with books. I made a note to check that room out later.

Turning to continue down the hall I almost bumped into a tall black woman that must've also been Native American. Her skin was darker than my dark brown skin and it shone with a brilliance that can only be produced by an abundance of melanin. The whites of her eyes were newborn baby white and her teeth were just as white if not whiter. Her nose was broad and powerful like pictures of Africans and Native Americans I'd seen in magazines. Her hair hung down long around her shoulders and down her back. She had a broad mouth that looked like it could laugh and laugh then quickly change to anger and maybe curse you.

Her eyes were somewhat slanted and dark brown, maybe black. With all that said, she exuded a wise motherly presence. She had on a house dress with a full apron over it. There was a dish cloth in her right hand and house shoes on her feet. I'd say she wore a size ten and had to be almost six feet tall compared to my five-foot five inches. Her neck was long and regal like the rest of her and her tear drop shaped face held all her features in place. In all her regalia her hands looked like she was accustomed to hard work. She looked to be in her late fifties to early sixties with many strands of silver decorating her jet black hair. Her gray feet were pushed into house shoes exposing her white heels. She was beautiful. She was also a little intimidating looking.

"I guess you must be the one I spoke to on the phone," she said. "Did you have any trouble getting here?"

"Uh, no, your directions were perfect," I responded. "I stopped by Manny's to pick up a few things before coming here."

"Oh, that explains it. So what are you doing in L.A.? You visiting family, going to school, what?" she asked leading me into the kitchen.

"Well," I said sitting my bag on the spacious counter, "I'm actually here pursuing a singing career."

"Oh really? I've encountered many girls your age that wanted to do the same thing," she said looking at me. "Where's your family," she asked as if she knew.

"They're back in Jersey," I answered looking through my shopping bag to escape her prying eyes.

"When are you going to call them to let them know you're ok?" she asked almost telling me.

"When I get around to it," I said getting upset that this woman was in my business uninvited. I wanted to tell her to mind her business and that I didn't need a second mother, but I hadn't yet been offered the room. Actually, I thought I'd better never get on that woman's bad side because she looked like she wouldn't think twice about kicking my butt out. I could see that she sensed my attitude. I made a note to soften my tone.

"When you get around to it? What kind of talk is that girl?" she asked. "Your mama needs to know where you are regardless of what the two of you think about each other," she demanded. I opened my mouth to speak but was cut off when she said, "She's probably looking for you."

What did she know? She thought she had me figured out. By this time arrogance showed up, but not too much when I said, "I just want to get settled, get my head together, and then let my parents know where I am."

Satisfied, she said, "B and C are available, C is the larger of the two, here's the key to C, let me know what you think after you take a look," she said with a look I couldn't identify, but I had the feeling she'd be even more in my business than I'd care for her to be.

She didn't bother to show me to the room and I didn't ask. Instead of taking the long hall we took to get to the kitchen I decided to take another hall off the side. As I walked down the hall I saw two bedrooms, one decorated in dark manly colors and the other in light female colors. The boarding house seemed more like a hotel or a bed and breakfast than what it was and was very comfortable and warm. On the other side of the hall there was a large dining room that had a long table that looked like it could seat twenty to twenty-five people. There was a white table cloth on it and it was already set.

I figured there must be about fifteen boarders after counting all the bedrooms. Getting my bearings, I found my way back to the stairs I saw when I first walked through the house, and ascended them. At the top of the stairs a long hallway lay before me and I passed a bathroom that had a male symbol on it then a room that was like a janitor's closet. It had cleaning products in it, shelves, mops, brooms, cloths, buckets and other things of that nature in it.

I passed room B, then I saw room C at the end of the hall after passing a ladies room that had a double sink, stall shower, bathtub, and two toilets in it! I was impressed to see all of those things in one bathroom and decided that the African-Indian woman was rich. I unlocked the door to room C and pushed it open. Sunlight poured into the room from four windows. The far left corner of the room had two windows on either side of the corner. The windows on the left of the corner faced the side of the house and the others faced the front of the house.

The windows facing the side of the house gave a view of the house next door and you could also see the railing outside attached to the upper level porch. There was a table situated in the same corner where the windows were and on the same side of the room but at the opposite wall there was a desk and chair. Behind me on the other side of the room near the hall door was a twin sized bed that had no sheets or blanket on it. Beside the bed was a nightstand with a lamp on it and on the other side of the bed there was a bookshelf with about two shelves that came up to my waist.

On the floor next to the bed where the nightstand was there was a red rectangular-shaped rug. A few pictures hung on the wall depicting different scenes from nature like a beautiful day that reminded me of Jersey in the early fall with red, yellow, and orange leaves covering the ground. Another picture was of the beach that made me think of the California I was used to seeing on television. The third picture looked like New York City or Chicago. I couldn't tell which because the buildings that were photographed weren't giving up enough clues. Snow fell on the city covering the street, sidewalks, and buildings. It was a peaceful picture although the city looked loud and busy.

All the floors upstairs were dark brown wood so the red rug next to my bed against the brown of the floor was beautiful. I already considered the room mine. When I turned around and walked to the door to step into the hall I saw the African-Indian woman making her way toward me with linen, a blanket, washcloths, and a towel.

"I take that you like the room," she said, "So I brought up some fresh linen and towels for you from the basement. My name's Marlene," she said firmly. "Some of the boarders call me, Ms. Marlene, Mary, Ms. Mary, whatever," she said. "Whatever you feel comfortable calling me along those lines is fine with me," she said smiling and handing me what was in her arms. "Oh, the room's $20.00 a week which includes your room and board and three meals a day. You're welcome to buy whatever snacks and things you like and keep them in your room as long as they're kept closed and don't smell, and your room is kept clean. I don't know if you noticed but there's another room up here with a refrigerator and freezer in it. You can keep your perishable foods in there and your non-perishables on the shelves if you choose not to keep them in your room. Oh, and there's a washer and dryer on this floor across the hall that take quarters. I make all the meals but if there's something you want that's not on the menu you're welcome to make it yourself. There's a curfew here in this house. If you come in after eleven during the week you get locked out and if you come in after one on the weekend you get locked out. No sex in my house. No overnight guests except for the same sex and you have to let me know about it first so I'll know what's going on. We do have some thieving around here from time to time so I advise you to lock your door behind you every time you leave. Since you and the other girl living up here have two doors you have two keys and have to keep an extra eye out. Breakfast is at seven Monday through Friday and nine on the weekends. Lunch is at noon everyday and dinner is served at six everyday. If you show up to meals

25

late that's up to you but you have no one to blame but yourself if there's nothing left. Maybe if you make a friend here he or she will make a plate for you if you're going to be late. Rent is due at the end of every week on Sunday in a box labeled "Rent" downstairs in the hall near the recreation room. On rent day, I check the box three times. The last time I check is around eleven just before lights out and if I don't have your rent in a sealed envelope in that box by then and you're not here then I'll assume you're not coming back. If it's not in the box by eleven and you are here then I'll assume you're getting ready to get out. Unless you have a legitimate excuse for not having your rent on time you will be put out. Anyone around here will tell you that I'm fair but I don't play when it comes to rent," she said, as her list of rules finally came to an end.

"Okay, I'll take it," I said.

"Good, since today is Tuesday, on Sunday you can pay me for six nights so I figure that's about $17.00."

"That's okay, I'll pay you for three months in advance. I just want to make sure I don't have to think about rent for a while," I said. I handed Marlene $240.00 and she pulled a receipt book out of an apron pocket, filled out a page, ripped it off, then handed it to me. We shook hands then she welcomed me and reminded me that dinner was at six.

"Oh, and another thing, you can listen to whatever you want to during the week but on Sunday I don't want to hear anything but gospel, classical, or something along those lines. I don't want to hear anything talkin' about baby I love you, I need you, I want you or whatever. Now I can't make you go to church, but this is my house and I can make my own rules."

"Okay, I understand," I said as Marlene walked away punishing the backs of her house shoes with every step. Now that I had a place to live taken care of I had to secure some form of income because I used some of the $3,000.00 I saved up to make the trip across country, at Manny's, and for the rent I'd given Marlene. Before I knew it, the rest of the money would be gone. I made my bed and laid my towel and washcloth on my desk. I opened my purse and pulled out the page from the want ads I was reading earlier.

I left my room to find the hall phone Marlene told me about so I could make a few calls. I found the phone in the room with the refrigerator in it and I started calling. I called in order of preference so I called the law firm first then the diner next.

Thankfully I was able to schedule both interviews for Thursday. That was two days away. That gave me a day to check out my new neighborhood and buy something to wear to the interviews. I went back to my room, closed the door behind me and sat down on my bed to take everything in. I thought about the talent show and how I had to prepare for it. I knew I was going to win so I didn't worry about that, but what I was concerned with was my hair, makeup, and an outfit.

I only had thirty minutes before dinner so I decided not to leave to check out the neighborhood, but it did give me some time to check out some of those rooms downstairs and maybe meet some of the other boarders. I remembered what Marlene said and put my purse in the drawer of my nightstand. I made sure the side door was locked and bolted. I walked out into the hall, locked my door and pulled it tight. I knelt down and put my room key in one of my shoes and kept walking.

Approaching the stairs, I smelled some wonderful things that reminded me of home. I knew I smelled fried chicken and some kind of vegetable flavor with smoked turkey, macaroni and cheese, and something sweet baking. I hoped it was sweet potato pie.

I felt something in my chest move. It was guilt and sadness. I still hadn't called my parents and it had been a week since I left home. I really didn't know what to say to them so I decided not to call anytime soon. I couldn't write because they'd see the postmark was from L.A. then the next thing I'd know I might run into them looking for me. Right then something told me that they may not react that way, that they're sorry and just want to know that I'm safe. I shook my head, stepped onto the main level, and continued exploring.

The other boarders were a rainbow of faces. There were blacks, whites, Hispanics, and Asians, but mostly blacks. Everyone got along too. I think I was one of the youngest there at the boarding house. I decided I was going to call it Marlene House.

Dinner was delicious. We all sat down at six except for those that helped out in the kitchen and placed the food on the table. It actually seemed more like Thanksgiving than a Tuesday night dinner. I don't know if everyone believed in Jesus or God or anything at all for that matter but when we were all seated Marlene gestured for us to hold hands then she bowed her head and everyone else did the same.

After Marlene said grace, we all dug in. After a while food began falling off my fork from the short trip from my plate to my mouth, and I was embarrassed. At that moment I noticed several pairs of eyes staring at me and I started feeling uncomfortable. I held eye contact with a few of them but then decided to just keep my eyes on my plate since I noticed a couple of the men and one of the women stealing food from other people's plate.

Marlene's eyes scanned the table the whole time, calling people on different things like chewing with their mouth open and smacking loudly yet overlooking some things like food stealing. She was like a mother hen or a lunch aide for a group of grown orphans.

Expectantly, Marlene's eyes finally fell on me then she cleared her throat and said, "I guess I have to be the one with manners around here since no one cares to introduce himself to our new boarder. Everyone at this table was new to this house at one time or another so you know how it is whether you care or not." Standing up and taking her napkin from her lap she said, "Everyone this is Diane," then she pointed to everyone at the table and said their name and how long they'd been living there.

Some of them spoke in between mouthfuls, some waved, and a couple never looked up from their plate. There were more men than women and more older adults than young. There were sixteen of us at the table including Marlene. After dinner as I walked into the kitchen to rinse my dishes, a twenty-something looking woman hooked her arm into my left arm and said, "Why don't you come to the rec. room down the hall when you're done."

She was cute. She looked like Gladys Knight to me. She had the same cute nose, lips, and eyes. She really looked like they were close relatives. Her hair was dark brown and straightened. It fell just below her chin and was flipped upward at the ends. She was about my height and had on a tee-shirt, jeans, and a pair of platforms. She and I had similar taste in clothes and I liked her immediately.

"Okay," I said then she smiled and walked away. When I was through in the kitchen I walked to the threshold of the rec. room and scanned it for my hopefully new friend.

"Hey girl," she said meeting me at the door. "I know you probably forgot already but its okay. My name is Carla," she said, while she led me to the back right corner of the room toward two chairs and a coffee table. We sat down and Carla told me her story.

She was twenty-three years old and had been living in L.A. for three years. She moved to L.A. from Ohio because she wanted to be an actress. She'd gotten a few small parts here and there but nothing to set her career off to the next level. She said although things seemed to be pretty slow she was hopeful and had faith that she'd be the next Pam Grier.

We both laughed when she said the part about Pam Grier. I told her she could do anything and that I believed in her. I shared my dream with her and she encouraged me as well. We became fast friends visiting each other's room and talking late into the night. She told me where to buy a nice outfit for my interviews and she even helped me find something cute for the talent show.

I went to both interviews and both jobs had good and bad points. The legal assistant gig was more my style because it was in a big, modernly designed building and I had to get dressed up everyday for work. The hours were nine-to-five, I would have an hour paid lunch, lots of shops to visit during lunch, and the attorney I'd be working for was nice, plus the office was small, which was also a plus.

Now for the bad parts. The attorney was nice. Too nice I might add. He was married but was interested in having something on the side with me and wasn't shy about letting me know it. He was harmless though, asking if I wanted to go to lunch after the interview, or dinner, if I could come back after the office closed. He said if I stayed he'd drive me home. I really couldn't believe how desperate he was as I looked at all the degrees and awards on his wall.

My eyes roamed his desk and stopped on the picture of his wife. She looked like she was in her fifties and really didn't look all that bad. She needed a makeover though. A new hairstyle, some more obvious makeup, maybe some hair color, and she could tweeze those unruly eyebrows and chin hairs, and lose a little weight. Then she'd be good to go.

As the attorney rambled on about the job and what my responsibilities would be I took a good look at him. He was overweight and had on glasses that looked like they hadn't been cleaned in months. The buttons on his shirt over his beer belly were screaming to be set free and his hair reminded me of George Jefferson's from the old TV show "The Jeffersons". He probably started stepping out on his wife because she let herself go a little. My goodness, they had five kids.

I wondered when was the last time he took a good look in the mirror. He probably thought he looked good. I found that to be funny how a lot of men expect women to have babies and lose the weight immediately so they look like they never had kids but they can walk around looking a mess. They want their woman to look good for them but when it comes to them getting in shape it doesn't apply.

With the interview over, we stood up to shake hands and he came from around his desk to eye me over one more time then I left with a business card that had his personal numbers on it. I decided not to take the job although I believe I had the job the moment I walked through the door. My second interview was scheduled an hour later and was in the same part of town. I walked into the diner dragging my feet because I really didn't want to bother speaking with anyone about the lousy position, but since I'd already forgotten about the other one, I went for it.

The diner was clean and in order unlike a lot of diners I'd been to. I felt overdressed the moment I laid eyes on my interviewer/owner/cook/ whatever needed to done around there. I was astonished that the place was so orderly despite the lack of help he had. It was weird though. There was a certain feel about the place that it was smack dab in the middle of being held in order and total chaos breaking out. It was as if everything was just waiting for one little thing to fall out of place then everything would fall apart.

"Okay," he said, "It's like this. You probably already know waitresses and waiters don't make a lot an hour, so the majority of what you make comes from tips. You said you don't have waitressing experience so I'll teach you. You have to be willing to jump in and do whatever needs to be done even if it's not in your job description. If you can work with this you've got the job and can start ASAP, today even. If not, you can go."

I sat there for a moment and his face hollered, "Well, what are you gonna do?!"

"Okay, I'll take it," I said.

"Can you start today?" he asked. My mind raced a bit before I said yes and he told me to follow him to the back. In a room off the kitchen he had aprons and other supplies stored. He looked at me really quick and handed me a waitressing dress, hair net, apron, order book, and a pen. He looked at me again and said, "Don't worry, you'll be fine. After today you'll feel like a pro. If anyone and I mean anyone gives you any trouble, stop what you're doing and come get me. Oh, by the way, my name is Dave. My wife Anna is usually here but she's out running an errand," he said grabbing supplies from the shelf, turning the light off and leaving me in the dark room to shut the door behind me.

"The bathrooms are over there. We don't have a break room so we lock our personal things up in the supply room you were just in," he said rushing around the kitchen. "This is the kitchen. We were just in the supply room. There's the freezer," he said opening and closing it. "There's the dining room," he said doing a sweeping action with is arm.

By this time it was three o'clock. We didn't discuss hours or anything but I decided to stay a few hours to get the feel of things then I'd leave.

I expected things to pick up a little around five or six but it was outrageous how packed the place got. Thankfully Anna made it back about fifteen minutes after I began taking orders. She and Dave rushed around like two maniacs and before I knew it I was doing the same thing and my feet couldn't take it any longer.

After the rush calmed down Anna came to me and introduced herself. She told me that I did very well and that I could go home and soak my feet. She also suggested I wear a pair of sneakers the next day. I grabbed my things from the supply closet as I was on my way through the kitchen. Just before entering the dining area Anna handed me a plastic bag with a platter of food inside.

"I noticed you didn't eat anything while you were out there so I made you a plate of spaghetti and garlic bread," she said. "I didn't know what you'd prefer but I felt spaghetti was safe," she said smiling warmly.

I wearily returned her smile as I took the bag then put my jacket on and walked to my car. Inside I held onto the steering wheel for a few moments and laid my head on it. My first day was tiring and it wasn't even a whole shift. I thought about calling that attorney back to ask if I could start in the morning. I started my car and drove off. When I got to Marlene House it was a little after eight at night.

To my surprise Carla met me in the front hall. I suppose she'd been sitting in the den waiting for me. "Girl, where you been?" she asked. "I thought you split or something or maybe something bad happened to you," she said hitting me on the shoulder. It felt good to have a friend and I hadn't been in L.A. for a whole week yet.

"Naw, I'm okay," I said. "Remember, I told you about my two interviews, well, I went to them and ended up working a few hours," I said.

"Oh, yeah? That's slammin," Carla said. "So which one hired you?"

I told her all about the attorney and his high hopes and about David, Anna, and the diner.

"Sounds nice but I know you can't be bringing home a lot of bread waitressing," she said following me up the stairs to my room. Dragging my feet I walked down the hall to my door and unlocked it.

"Girl you look beat," Carla said sitting at the foot of my bed as I lay across it on my face.

"I am," I whined with my voice muffled through my pillow. "I can't believe how tired I am. I mean this is the job I said yes to and now I'm going pay for choosing the wrong gig," I said imagining more grueling days ahead.

"Listen Diane, all you have to do is start looking for another job. Get some more newspapers and go to interviews on your break. You know you'll get hired then you can quit working at the diner," she said.

"Yeah you're right. I'm going to have to do that," I said. "But I'm not going to be doing these types of jobs for long anyway because after I win the talent show I'll be on tour with Trevor and his band and I won't have to worry about this job stuff."

"Listen, I really think you have a great voice and you have the look and personality to match, but it ain't that easy trying to make it out here. I'm glad you're mature enough to go out and get a job because lots of people come here expecting to get rich and famous as soon as they step foot in L.A. then they get a rude awakening when they realize there's so many people out here already with just as much talent, if not more, doing what they came here to do. It's tough sis."

"Hey I realize that but I gotta try because if I don't then I'll never know if I could've made it. I know I have what it takes but I have to convince the people that matter that I do."

"Girl, you sound just like me when I first stepped off the bus and took a look around. I knew someone would either approach me on the street because of my undeniable beauty or they'd be mesmerized by my acting ability at an audition. Even though I want you to continue encouraging yourself and being your own cheerleader, you have to be brave enough to know when you've spent enough time moving in one direction. Let me tell you that I feel like giving up sometimes, but I've given myself a deadline. If I don't make it big by the time I'm thirty or thirty-five, I'm throwing in the towel."

"I've read that some stars have spent longer than that waiting for their big break and then one day it finally happens."

"I know, I know, but look at what they have to go through to get there," she said stretching herself out and leaning on her elbows.

"Well, I know they had to sacrifice a lot and some were even homeless before everything changed for them," I said turning over and looking up at the ceiling.

"Do you know what most of these stars out here had to do to get that dream role or signed to a label?" she asked getting really serious.

"They put in a lot of hard work, energy, and..."

"Girl, please," she said rolling her eyes. "They had to sleep their way to the top and that's the only way a lot of celebrities, male and female made it. It had nothing to do with their talent, their look, or their voice, because all that mattered was what they were willing to do, and you know what I mean," she said lowering her voice to a whisper and raising her eyebrows.

I felt a little embarrassed that I didn't know about all that so I acted like I'd heard about it but just didn't believe it.

"Oh, I know all about that," I lied. "I just thought it wasn't happening as much these days," I said trying to redeem myself.

"Are you kidding me? It's only going to get worse. These producers and directors and whoever else, dangle success in front of everyone out here who's struggling to get noticed but it comes with a price," she said in a matter of fact tone.

"Well, how do you know so much about this subject? I mean I know you have acting friends and you're pursuing it too, but you seem to have some insight like it happened to you or someone close to you," I prodded.

Moving closer to me she said, "Remember the small part I got in that soap opera I told you about?"

"Yeah. I remember seeing you in a commercial promoting that episode. You looked great."

"Well, I had to do more than audition to get that small part. The producer told me point blank one day in his office that if I wanted the leading role I had to go away with him for the weekend. But because I refused I was picked for that small part and eventually written off."

"I thought you said you had to do something to get the part," I said realizing she'd left something out.

"Oh," she said. "We went out a few times to dinner and to a few clubs but after the third night out he started to get touchy- feely with me like he'd earned the right to do it. I mean we kissed a few times and stuff but when he wanted to go further I said no. He asked me if I realized who he was and I said, "Of course I do, you're Nathan Alstein who thinks he can have anyone in Hollywood that he wants because he thinks he's God."

After that he told me that I better find another craft because I was finished as an actress. I told him I didn't need him in order to make it and he laughed at me. He told me the offer was an open invitation and anytime I wanted to take my career seriously," she said making quotation marks with her fingers, "all I had to do was call him. I still have his business card," she said.

"But I can't bring myself to do it. I can't sell myself for fame like that.

I'm worth more than that," she said as she pulled the business card out of her shirt pocket. "I can't lie though. Sometimes I get so depressed and so mad with myself that I come close to calling him to get it over with. My agent keeps getting me auditions but they're either movies that Nathan Alstein is producing or directing or he's connected to someone else's project in some way. I know he has everything to do with why I can't get any work," she said with a sigh.

I thought about what she said as I examined the card she handed me. The card felt like silk in my hand and I loved the feel of the letters beneath my fingers. "Wow," I said. "That's deep," as I wondered about my future as a singer.

CHAPTER 4

Diane

I sure didn't see this coming...

My second day at work was just as busy if not busier than the first because it was Friday. Anna and I took care of customers like robots and bussed tables one after the other. Before I left for home I told Anna about the talent show I was going to attend in a week and asked if I could get off early the day before. She told me I could work half a day. That weekend, I worked Saturday but had off on Sunday so Carla and I went shopping.

We checked out so many stores that I was exhausted by the time we got back to Marlene House. We had several bags for ourselves and had lunch and laughed and talked. We had a really nice time and I could tell that Carla would be a good friend.

I ended up buying a wig with deep waves in it. It was sexy, black and came to my shoulders. I found a short green sequence dress with spaghetti straps to wear. Carla said it was provocative and I think that's the extra push I needed to buy it since it cost $200.00. Last, I bought a pair of heels to match. We even stopped by a boutique to pick up some makeup and fake lashes.

I was excited and kept picturing myself on the stage dazzling the crowd and the judges and most of all Trevor. I imagined hearing my name being called as the winner after all the runners up were named. I stepped forward to take the bouquet of flowers as the audience chanted "Di-an, Di-an, Di-an! Diane we love you!"

When my mind returned to my room Carla was still talking about how she managed to free up her schedule in order to see the talent show.

"Oh that's great Car," I said calling her by the nickname I'd given her. "Can you take pictures of me on stage singing and accepting my bouquet?"

"Sure," she said hesitantly, as we stepped into the hall to go to dinner.

℘

Tuesday evening after work I went up to my room to change and relax. I pulled out the plate of food I made myself and sat down at my table to eat and look out the window at the street. I was very tired and wanted to go to sleep. Before bed I had to take a shower and I just didn't feel like it, but I pulled myself up somehow and went to the hall bathroom to wash away the diner smell.

I hadn't spoken with Carla all day so I planned to stop by her room afterward to say hi. Carla's room was next door to the bathroom so I could take my shower, then stop by Carla's room on my way back to my room. While I was washing my face at the sink I could hear Carla talking to someone. I couldn't quite make out what the conversation was about but I know she was talking to a woman.

Listening more intently, I still didn't know what they were saying but from the tone of their voices it was a serious conversation about something important that involved at least one of them if not both. I heard more urgency coming from Carla's visitor and I got the impression she was the one with the problem and came to Carla for help.

I stepped into the shower and could hear nothing over the drumming of the water. After I dried off and put on my robe I heard Carla's door open and close and footsteps leaving her room but not to the hall. They were leaving through Carla's other door that lead to the porch outside. Feeling nosy I hurried back to my room and turned my light off so I could peek through the blinds to see who was with Carla.

First I saw Carla's visitor. She was dressed like she was going to go out with friends for the night. She was Latino with long dark hair down her back that hung straight and free. She had a certain vibe about her that at the time I didn't pinpoint. She wore heavy makeup and her lips were so red they looked bloody. Carla followed wearing a pair of jeans and a short sleeved tee-shirt with a black power fist on it. She looked like she usually does so nothing struck me out of the ordinary except Carla had her hands on the girl's back like she was hurrying her from the house. As they passed my window, I heard Carla say between clenched teeth, "I told you never to come here no matter what!"

The girl responded, "I know but I had to come over because I didn't have anyone else to go to."

Okay, so Carla had something going on and I wondered what it was. I didn't think too much of it though because Carla and I were still getting to know each other. That girl could've been one of her acting friends or one of her friends from work. Besides I had my own business to contend with. Whatever was going on I was sure it wasn't anything. I decided to ask Carla about it later...maybe.

🙖

I had the perfect hair, outfit, and makeup but I was still trying to decide what song to mesmerize the crowd and judges with. I just knew Trevor would be thoroughly impressed with my singing ability. I didn't know whether I should sing something slow like *Killing Me Softly with His Song* or something a little more up tempo like *Respect*. Both would showcase my talent but in different ways, however, I wanted everyone to get everything I had to offer. Once I decided which song to sing I had to find a place to rehearse. I definitely couldn't rehearse at Marlene House but I didn't know where else to go.

Just then, I heard footsteps heading toward the stairs and onto the landing of the upper porch. I was still looking into the darkness until the flickering light on the corner of the house shined bright, and Carla appeared coming toward my window quickly. I snatched my hand away from the blinds, ran across my room to the bed, and jumped on it. I bounced up and down so hard I hit my head on the headboard. I heard Carla's side door creak open then close and I listened for a while. Hearing nothing, I got up, put on a nightgown and got back into bed falling fast asleep.

The next morning, I saw Carla in the bathroom and she seemed fine so I didn't ask her about the night before. That night after work, as I was approaching the top of the stairs Carla stuck her head out of the laundry room and asked me to come in. She was all smiles while she unloaded the dryer.

"Girl, guess what?!" she asked excitedly.

"What?!" I asked even more excited.

"My agent got me an audition with Michael Cicazzo, you know, the guy who produced that movie about some teenagers that broke out of juvie, formed a gang then went around the city recruiting other teens, then they ended up warring with another gang over turf and stuff?"

"Yeah!" I said excited for her. "Tell me more!"

"Well, instead of a sequel they're going to make a movie based on one of the female gang members that meets a woman that convinces her that she can have a better life. After that she tries to get out of the gang although she knows that once she's in, she's in for life."

"Okay, okay, I remember the part where she was jumped. She was jacked up and I thought she was dead, but when I saw her move a little and try to get up I was so happy," I said. "I felt like I knew her. That's how real she seemed. The girl who played that part did a great job," I said recollecting the movie.

"Yeah, I know and I'm auditioning to play the part of the same girl several years later," she said jumping up and down and clapping.

"Wow!" I said genuinely happy for her. "That's out of sight girl! I'm really happy for you! I see all your hard work has paid off. I know you'll do a great job and you'll get the part hands down," I said.

"And guess what?" she asked, the news getting better and better. "I'm getting a private audition for the part before the producer and the director and if they like me, they'll end the casting call immediately for that part and I'll leave the audition knowing I've got it!"

"Carla that's great!" I said becoming weary from hearing all her good news. I had two more nights until my big break and I was getting more nervous by the hour. I was surprised at my sudden behavior but I suppose the reality of it all was setting in. I was so close to becoming the star, the entertainer, the household name that I came to L.A. to be.

I told Carla how happy I was again and congratulated her then walked to my door and opened it. Walking in and turning around to lock the door I realized I felt a tinge of envy thinking about Carla and her opportunity. I had to check myself though because she'd been pursuing acting for several years and I'd just begun putting my time in. I ended up asking for all day Thursday and Friday off because I needed time to pull my act together and pick the song that would change my life forever.

The evening Carla invited me to the den she confided that the basement of Marlene's house has a lot of stuff in it but she sometimes goes down there to be alone even though she has the privacy of her own room. She realized one day that you can barely hear someone screaming down there from upstairs. She said she knows this because a couple years ago Marlene somehow got locked down there and said she was screaming for hours for someone to open the door until dinner time rolled around and some of the boarders started looking for her because she hadn't begun dinner. That gave me the idea to practice in the basement.

I told Carla I'd be down there Thursday and Friday just in case I got

38

locked down there. She doubted I would since Marlene had a locksmith come in and change the lock on the door because she was terrified of the thought of being locked down there again. I finally decided on singing *Killing Me Softly with His Song* which came after rehearsing a total of six hours over the two days I gave myself to practice, because I didn't want to damage my throat.

Just a few hours before the talent show was to start I began to get ready, taking a nice long, hot shower, applying lotion, perfuming myself, and doing my makeup. Then there was a knock at my door that was unfamiliar to me. I asked who it was and I was surprised that it was Marlene. I opened the door and she asked to come in. I said yes and she walked over to the bed and sat down. She then did something that seemed very unlike the Marlene I'd come to know over the past week. When she sat down she patted the space beside her indicating that she wanted me to sit.

Okay, what's this about? I thought as I sat down facing her.

"I know you're going to the talent show in a bit and I want you to do your best. I don't know that much about you because you're so new, but from watching you, you remind me of someone I know very well – myself."

Sitting there looking at Marlene I wondered how in the world this woman could see herself in me. What about us was similar to her?

"You're determined to win the talent show and although I've never heard you sing I see something in your eyes that tells me you possess that something special that will enable you to go far with the gift God gave you," she said looking so intently at me that it scared me a little. I didn't understand why she was being so tender. It was as if she cared about me. I quickly pushed that thought from my mind knowing good and well that Marlene had some of the boarders afraid of her although we all lived like a family. It was weird.

I'd never really thought much about God growing up even after moving across the country. I still didn't think about God other than saying grace and giving God thanks when something worked out for me. I'd heard some people say that my voice was a gift from God whenever I sang, but their words never meant anything to me or made me think about what they were saying.

Growing up mom and dad taught me to say grace, little children's prayers, and we went to church for weddings, funerals, Christmas, Easter, and sometimes for New Year's Eve, but not every Sunday like Celeste's family. Celeste's mom and dad were active in church and talked to us about God all the time. I even went to a few overnight slumber parties at her church that were actually fun.

The youth leaders talked to us about things like peer pressure to do drugs, have sex, join gangs, and a lot of other things that we dealt with in high school. I thought those slumber parties were fun because at some point during the night we'd all get on the church bus and go to a bowling alley or skating rink.

The youth leaders told us that it's important to have a personal relationship with Jesus Christ because He loves us and that God said no man can come to Him except through His Son who is Jesus. The only Bible verse I know is John 3:16 where it says that God loves the world so much that He sent Jesus and that whoever believes in Jesus won't go to hell but have eternal life in Heaven. Those aren't the exact words but that's what the verse means.

I still don't know how I feel about that because you have to trust the fact that God is real in the first place, and once you determine that you believe He exists then you have to believe that Jesus exists and that he was sent to earth to save mankind from his sins even though He didn't have to. But He wanted to because He loves us.

I hated that Marlene made me remember God because thinking about God made me feel funny like I had to do something. I felt some type of guilt. Hearing Marlene mention God made me feel uncomfortable and I had enough to be concerned with than to be thinking about whether God truly exists in a world that claims many gods. Marlene had to get out of my room.

"Uh, Marlene thanks for the encouragement. It means a lot to me," I said rudely standing up and walking over to the door. Marlene looked at me with an expression on her face that could've said many things. It was sort of an all purpose expression that could say, "Who do you think you're talking to?, I wasn't finished talking to you, or I've been where you're going and I have a few pointers for you but since you so rudely interrupted me you can go on out there and see for yourself."

"Okay, I just want you to know that I'll be praying for you and God willing you'll win," Marlene said standing up. She patted me on the back before stepping into the hall and walking off. Before I closed my door and she reached the stairs, she turned around quickly and asked me if I called my parents yet. I told her no and closed the door.

I read on a flyer for the talent show that all contestants had to show up or call three days in advance to register. They took three hundred contestants and somehow eliminated some each night. The contest was set to start that day then would continue Saturday and through the following Friday. The last day of the contest was the day all the finalists were to compete. Each contestant that wasn't eliminated was given a number and that's the order each finalist was expected to perform in the following Saturday and the winner was scheduled to be announced that night. I didn't remember hearing all that on the radio back in Jersey but whatever had to be done I was willing to do it.

I'd never participated in a talent show that had so many people involved and took place over so many days. I hated the fact that it wouldn't be over that night. I absolutely hated it. I hated the pressure. I've always been one to go ahead and get stressful situations over with. As I sat in class taking an exam that I knew nothing about I'd check over my answers and just turn it in. Looking at the test until class was over wasn't going to make me know what I didn't.

I could remember the nervousness I felt before my first ever talent show. I could hear everyone in the auditorium talking and it seemed like the talking just got louder and louder until finally my name was called. Sweaty hands and all, I took a deep breath as I walked out on stage. Standing there with the spotlight on me my heart fluttered with fear and excitement until only excitement pumped through me.

Looking at myself one last time in the bathroom mirror I blew myself a kiss and said a low *"good luck"* to my reflection and headed for the stairs. On my way to the door I saw a few heads turn then I pulled it shut behind me.

Once I reached the building where the event was going to take place I saw other girls and some guys walking across the street. People of all races, shapes, and sizes crossed the street before me. I saw some beautiful people walking into that building and it intimidated me. I checked my reflection in the rearview mirror one last time. Ready or not I stepped out of my car and joined a group of people herding across the street.

Male and female took the stage one after the other. Some were a total disgrace to all that sounded lovely while others wowed even me. I wondered who encouraged the others to get on stage to compete with people that weren't tone deaf and could actually sing. Right and left people were dismissed. Male and female, young and old, beautiful and not so beautiful left the stage in tears, with their face in their hands, or with a cloud of curses behind them. When it was my turn I took the stage and focused on the judges in the audience ahead of me. I noticed the small audience that had come to watch was made up of some of the people that were dismissed or given a number to perform the following Saturday night. If I was dismissed I wouldn't dare sit in the audience.

I stated my name and where I was from. I mentioned nothing about New Jersey. I said Los Angeles, CA. No one received instrumental accompaniment. That was alright with me. I closed my eyes and began to sing the first verse. A few moments later I opened them for fear that singing with my eyes closed might be a mark against me. I continued the song hitting every last note and holding until the song was finished.

"Fifteen," was all that was said to me by a judge but I did hear a few "Go on girls and go 'head do your things" from people in the audience and it was encouraging.

I walked to the judge to receive my piece of paper with the number fifteen printed in bold typed font on it and said "Thank you so much," as I reached for it. I reminded myself that there were six days between me and my dream. Six days compared to the fourteen years that I'd looked forward to living my dream became nothing. Ever since I was four years old I knew I wanted to sing. I decided to celebrate so I stopped by an ice cream shop and bought myself a hot fudge sundae. Sitting there I realized that Carla never showed up. She told me she'd be there. I felt a little disappointed and curious as to why she wasn't there. Something must've come up. Something more important than supporting a friend I supposed.

Back at Marlene House I entered my room, locked my door, and began to undress. I'd peeked up the darkened hall and saw no light under Carla's door. She either wasn't in or she was asleep. It was not so late at ten o'clock. After taking a shower I sat up in bed with my thoughts. I had to be realistic and face the fact that everything doesn't happen when and how you want it. I felt myself doubting my ability to win the contest, but I wasn't going to give my parents the satisfaction. I then decided not to call them until after I won the talent show and could tell them "I told you so". They never believed in me so I wasn't going to let them know where someone they don't believe in or support was. They could continue wondering where I was for another week. It wouldn't hurt them.

Work did very little to keep my mind off my future because Anna kept asking me questions about it. I tried not to show that I'd rather do anything than that, because Anna was such a sweet person, so I answered every question she had. I caught up with Carla mid-week who apologized for not showing up but she had a good excuse not to. She said she'd gotten the role and was getting to know everyone that she'll be working with. She talked to me about actors and actresses that I'd only seen on television then she pulled out some pictures of her laughing and eating with them!

"Wow!" I said. "You just got the part and already you're partying with them!" Jealousy crept up my spine and I straightened up my posture to push it back down. I noticed something different about her. She had on some expensive clothes and her hair had been done. Her skin seemed to glisten and her polished nails shone bright. I was officially attacked by the green eyed monster. The next thing I'd know Carla would be able to afford a condo or a mansion or something and I'd still be at Marlene House wishing I was with her.

∾

Well, I ended up bumping into Marlene Friday night despite all the attempts I made to avoid her. I think she realized what I was doing and must've snuck up on me.

"Listen, I don't know why I'm doing this. Well, yes I do, but I don't know why I care," she said after cornering me in the upstairs laundry room. "Carla is bad news. You think she's your friend but she's not. She doesn't even know how to be a friend to herself. You better listen to me girl," she said flaring her nostrils. She looked like she was mad at me. I really didn't understand Marlene. I brushed past her with my arms filled with warm, just dried clothes and stomped to my room like I was having a tantrum.

That's one of the things that upset me about Marlene. First, she was getting in my business, next she was acting like she was my mother. Just as I kicked out my right foot behind me to shut the door, Marlene put her big foot in the way and blocked it so it wouldn't close.

"You're going to wish you never met Carla," she said then walked away.

I slammed my door not understanding why I allowed Marlene to get to me the way she did. If Carla was such bad news then why did she allow bad news to live under her roof? I suppose it was because bad news money is all the same to her and she kept her nose out of all the other boarder's business and limited her comments about their personal issues. I figured I had to change the way I dealt with Marlene. She just didn't bother with anyone else. Why was I the only one she was riding? It wasn't cool. In no way was it cool. As soon as I got a chance to I was going to check the paper for more boarding houses. I left one mother three time zones behind me and I wasn't about to be putting up with another. Especially one that thought she knew me and didn't have a clue of what I was about.

While pushing Marlene out of my mind, I thought about the contest. One thing I noticed is that only a few contestants were dressed up. Most of them came out in bell bottoms, tee-shirts, and platforms. It was cool though because they looked more comfortable and they grooved like it too. I noticed some of the others that came dressed up like me pulling on stockings and checking them for runs, making sure their skirts were straight and turned the right way while the guys were checking their ties and things. I made a decision to go comfortable too so I pulled out a pair of hip huggers, a cute tube top that fit just right, and I combed out my two big cornrows and picked my hair into a fro.

Saturday, my big day finally came and Carla was actually home. She even rode with me to the show. When we got there a handsome guy was leaning against the building smoking a cigarette. He was tall and medium built with an olive brown complexion, dark wavy hair and the brownest eyes that were topped by thick eyebrows that made him look a little mysterious. He smiled at us as we crossed the street approaching him. He took one last drag from his cigarette, flicked it to the ground and stepped on it. He blew out the smoke and reached out to Diane hugging her and kissing her full on the lips.

"Hi," he said to me and all I could do was wave and stutter a hello back.

"Oh Diane, this is Adam," she said as they walked hugging each other close to the side like lovers. Once inside I checked in and made my way behind the stage. After everyone was settled one of the judges got on a microphone and announced that the decision was made to have each contestant choose a song from a jar. He said by putting us on the spot they could really see our talent. All the songs were well known and since we got to choose a song prior to stepping on stage we had about two minutes each to rehearse the words before our name was called.

I got nervous after hearing about all the changes. It was just my luck that things would be rearranged like that. I don't know how many talent shows I've been to but I've never heard of all this mess going on. When it was my turn I stepped up to the table and reached inside the glass vase pulling out a tiny folded piece of paper. On it was a song that I remember hearing called *It's Not the Right Time*. I began humming the melody and smiled thinking I could definitely work it. My confidence crept back up and I began to sing a little louder, sure that I'd do great.

When number fifteen was called, I stepped out on stage and saw Carla and Adam all hugged up several rows from the front. I took a deep breath and did what I do best. Once the song was over Carla and Adam clapped and whooped and hollered for me. I saw the judges nod and they huddled together quickly then moved back to their places and wrote something down on a card.

About an hour later the contest was over. All of the finalists stood on stage obviously nervous and excited at the same time. Then, like the voice of God someone announced the winners.

"The third runner up prize goes to….. Danielle Tarver!" My heart skipped a beat at hearing the *d* in Danielle's name called. Danielle stepped out of line to claim her prize of $2,000.00. She was so happy, she cried. How could she be happy knowing that out of the three people chosen the judges liked her singing the least?

"The second runner up prize of $5,000.00 goes to Diane…" After hearing my first name I didn't hear anything else. I couldn't hear anything else. I couldn't move. I thought that if I didn't move it wouldn't be real. One of the girls next to me elbowed me and said, "They said your name," and nudged me a little. Everyone clapped and said congratulations as I walked by each of them to claim my second place prize. I felt like I had a glazed look on my face and I heard someone say that I looked like I couldn't believe I won.

I tried to change the expression on my face as I reached out to take the check. After all, I didn't want anyone to think I was ungrateful. I walked over to the other side of the stage to stand next to the girl the judges liked the least, and then the area behind my eyes began to burn. Tears pooled at the bottom of my eyes until I could no longer stand the pressure. Then huge crocodile tears fell one after the other as an uncontrollable sob escaped from deep within me. Carla and Adam stood and clapped and hoorayed for me but I was hurt because I couldn't do anything about the judge's decision. I had a mind to walk off the stage but then it would be obvious how I truly felt.

Finally, the winner was named. I remembered seeing her but I felt I had a better voice than she had. I was definitely more talented and way prettier than she was. She wasn't even a contestant I considered to be competition. It didn't matter what I felt though. The contest came to an end and I walked backstage to get my purse. When I stepped offstage Carla and Adam were waiting for me, but I didn't feel like being bothered with them. First of all they were grinning from ear to ear. The fact that they were in love was sickening to me, because I didn't want to see anyone happy because it seemed I'd never be. Walking up to them I fought walking right by them rushing to my car and driving off to be alone with my broken heart. I hated feeling so emotional and filled with tears and having the immense need to allow them to pour out but I had to hold them in the best I could.

I struggled physically to hold them back. It was harder than trying to keep one from slipping when you're surrounded by people. "*Quick, quick, quick*" I told myself as I tried to think of something else to take my mind off my devastation. I realized if I could just be quiet and not have to say anything then I'd be okay until I reached my car. Carla and her man were standing in front of me and I was there a statue of fragments only held together with pride. Little did they know that the least word could cause me to collapse.

"Hey mama," Carla said hugging me and bumping me with her hip. "You did great up there!" she said.

"Yeah baby you were on fire!" Adam said looking at me a moment too long. Carla noticed the look and for a split second I thought I saw a little jealousy. I ignored the awkward moment and focused on Carla. There was no way she could be jealous of me. Not Carla. Sensing my true feelings Carla put her arm around me as we continued to walk to the exit.

"Hey listen, I know you're not happy that you came in second place. But you've only been in L.A. two weeks and already you've almost won one of the biggest talent shows in California. Don't let this make you give up. I've been out here for several years and I've just landed the role of my dreams. You need to just put a little more time in," she said. Marlene was wrong about Carla. Carla wasn't bad news. She was sweet, seemed honest, and she was supportive and kind. Marlene was wrong. She was the one that was bad news. Since I was feeling a little better, Carla and Adam invited me out, but I chose to go home and lay down after the contest despite all Carla and Adam's coaxing to get me to go along with them.

On the way home, I grabbed another paper to check for a new place to live and maybe a new job. When I walked into Marlene House everyone was hanging around as usual. I was thankful for that. I was glad no one but Carla and Marlene knew I was in the contest. I was glad that I didn't have to tell everyone that I failed. That I didn't win. Some help God was. I wonder if Marlene even prayed. Well, if she didn't oh well, because I hadn't heard Carla nor a lot of other successful people say anything about God and they were just fine.

Why should I care anything about God anyway when I've done fine without Him for eighteen years, my parents even longer? If God loved and cared for me like Celeste's parents said then why don't I have parents that believe in my dream? Why did I have to leave home the way I did, and why didn't I win the contest? If God knows all things then He should've known how important the contest was to me and I should've won.

I didn't want to see Marlene but as was her new habit she popped up out of nowhere to get into my business.

"I guess things didn't go so well, huh?" she asked. I can't stand people that state the obvious when nothing really needs to be said, but I responded to her question.

"Um, no and yes," I said trying hard not to roll my eyes and continue walking while ignoring her. "I didn't win but I did come in second place," I said forcing out every word. I imagined myself retelling the same story to Anna and Dave. It's at times like that you kind of wish that every person you know that may possibly want to know what happed to you is in the same room at the same time so you only have to tell the story once.

"Well, there will be others and second isn't bad. At least you were a finalist," she said. Seeing an opportunity to vent instead of argue I said, "Yes, second isn't bad but it's not the best. I did my best and it wasn't good enough. I can't take giving my best and not getting the best," I said wearily walking upstairs.

"God gave His best and doesn't always get our best in return," she replied with what I should've felt was wisdom.

Taking a deep breath to clear my head before speaking I said, "Marlene, everything that goes on in my life does not require a response from you that includes God. I am so tired of hearing about God."

Ignoring what I'd just declared Marlene said, "God's not tired of hearing about you, thinking about you, making a way for you, and whether you believe it not, loving you," she said following me to my room and standing in the doorway. After putting my purse and newspapers on the bed I stopped then turned around to see Marlene standing there in her fierce way with her arms crossed over her bosom. She raised her eyebrows as if to ask "Well, can I come in or not?"

I answered out loud to her silent request. "This is your house Marlene. You prove that to me almost every day by following me around and offering me advice that I don't ask for, and trying to push your God on me."

"Huh-ha!" she guffawed like Rodge from "What's Happening". "Girl, if you don't sound just like me my name is not Mar-lene! Oh my goodness you sound just like me!" she shouted too loud. Tired of hearing about she and I being so much alike or at one time being so much alike I shut my door and arrogantly invited her to sit on my bed which was really hers, in my room that was really hers, in the house that was hers. I looked at her and slowly rolled my eyes as I shook my head side to side wearily and asked with venom dripping from each word, "Marlene, what on earth do you see in me that was ever in you?"

"Hmph," she said standing up and she began to pace around the room. She shook her long index finger at me when she said, "Your determination reminds me of myself. But there are other things too. You're brazen, selfish, defiant, clueless, blind, ungrateful, and anything else I can remember being. I see me in you. I also met a woman like Carla that I wish I had never met. I used to wonder why my life was so hard. I know now. Oh how I wish I knew then what I know now," she said.

"Here she goes again," I said under my breath. "Talking about Carla."

"I know everything that goes on in this house regardless of how you think I'm only in your business. I know who's been kicked out by their wife or husband for cheating, who left home because they couldn't handle the responsibility, you name it I know it," she said. "I know something else too. Carla is a prostitute and a liar. I've seen her become friends with several girls that have come through here over the past several years and they're either walking the streets, somewhere feigning, or both. Oh she might've landed that role but she didn't do it the way you think and she won't keep it for long. Don't let her fool you. That Hispanic girl that was here one night last week was a girl that came to L.A. on a Greyhound from Texas somewhere. Sweet girl, shy, a little naïve, would help me around the house, went to school and everything. Then Carla came along like the devil in her and told her she could help her out and…"

"Marlene," I said cutting her off, "as interesting, creative, and sad your story is I don't want to hear it. Carla isn't here to defend herself and I'm not about to sit around talking about her," I said getting up to kick Marlene out.

Marlene walked over to the door and said, "I see that a fool is a fool whether it's the forties or the seventies," and she walked off.

"What did she mean by that?" I asked myself quietly. "I know she ain't calling me no fool," I said a little louder. It was just loud enough to satisfy my pride but low enough that Marlene probably didn't hear. "I can't believe she thinks Carla is a prostitute. Even if I did decide to believe Marlene

I'd still be wrong because I have no proof other than Marlene's perception of Carla, and I was not going to take her word for it." I concluded that Carla was alright with me until she showed me otherwise. I opened the newspaper and laid it across the foot of my bed and scanned it for a new room and a new job.

CHAPTER 5

James

This can only be God...

By the time I reached the other end of the country I'd seen several different states and ate at numerous diners, restaurants, and hotel lounges. I slept in an array of different hotels and found myself in California about two months later. I have to say that it was fun driving around not knowing where I was going and not having to worry about time or who's got to pee and fighting over radio stations. It was just me and my main man- God.

My relationship with God grew over the two month period I traveled to California. I spent time meditating on His Word and basking in His presence right in my truck. The Holy Spirit came upon me so powerfully once while I was driving that I had to pull over and get out of the truck to lift my hands and dance in place. I was free. It felt good to be free...free to be myself. I was experiencing God like I never had before and it was amazing. I wish I could feel that way all the time.

When I saw the welcome sign for Los Angeles, I was comforted by the great feeling of completion. I've always been the type of person who writes lists to keep track of my day to day to do's and long term plans- really whatever I needed to do for whatever reason I wrote it down. When I drove past the welcome sign I picked up my memo pad and drew a line through *Reach California safely*.

Although I had more than enough money to last for a while I was determined to rent a place to stay and find a job. I had enough money to buy my own property but because I didn't know how long I'd be in California I made up my mind that renting was smarter. After driving through L.A. for a while I stopped at a corner store to stretch my legs and get some information about the city. I grabbed a map, a hot dog, and something to drink.

Approaching the counter I noticed how beautiful the cashier was. But I wasn't sure of her age. Then I felt that familiar place in me open up and deep down I knew I needed to get better control of my flesh. I was well aware of my weakness for women but it was something I rarely mentioned in my prayers. Then, it was something I felt I had control over and stupidly I never brought it before God so the Holy Spirit could anoint me with self control. I didn't think it was a problem as long as I didn't act on my thoughts, but my mind became a virtual playground for all kinds of sexual thoughts. Eventually I let my mind roam freely from one thought to another, and from one mental picture to another thinking it was okay because I'm a man.

The cashier wore a sexy smile that I instantly took a mental picture of and tucked away in that place in my mind, where all the things I want to hold onto instead of giving to God are housed for later use. Those things I always feel tempted by and oftentimes succumb to and repent over and over for, but I really don't want to give them up. Those are the things I realized I was satisfied with as long as I was able to come up with an excuse for them. I didn't really want to change. The Holy Spirit convicted me. But I always had an excuse. I figured there were only a few things I needed to work on versus the long list of things I'd already overcome.

I smiled at her and told her I was new in town. She seemed shy. I knew I had her. I asked her if she could show me around town and that I could stop by when she got off. Just then a man I presumed to be her father came from the back somewhere and she hung her head. Her beautiful smile was gone. I understood. An overprotective father. Well, that's good. Ignoring his daughter now I turned to the man and said hello. I paid for my things and left the store.

I noticed the area I was in was a business district so I drove further until I saw homes and drove up and down each block. Some homes were for sale and others were for rent. Some appeared to be boarding houses which I wanted no part of, then I saw a sign in the yard of a nice looking two story home with a kept up yard. Outside I saw an attractive woman that looked to be in her mid-to-late forties kneeling down at her flower garden pulling weeds. There was fresh grass on the sidewalk and driveway indicating the yard was recently cut. The sign in the yard said she was looking for a boarder. I stopped my truck and walked over to her. She looked up at me and smiled, but kept on working.

"Hi, I'm here to speak with you about renting a room," I said bending down to her level to get eye contact.

51

"Oh?" she asked raising her brows.

"Uh, yeah. I just moved to L.A. from New Jersey and I'm looking for a place to live and a job," I said giving more information than necessary.

"Well, I can help you with a place to stay," she said, "but you're on your own looking for work. Come on in and I'll show you around. My last boarder moved out about two months ago after three years. I put an ad in the paper but no one has called. That's why I put the sign in the yard. You're actually the first person that's showed any interest. Maybe the room is meant for you," she said winking.

"Yeah, maybe," I said following her through a side door into the kitchen. The kitchen was spotless. That concerned me because I didn't want to live in someone's house that would be on me about every little thing. I wanted to live in a clean place but not with a clean freak. We saw all the rooms on the first floor then we came to the basement which she explained to be the area for rent.

We walked down twelve steps to a large finished basement. The walls were wood paneled and there was a little kitchen area with a small counter and appliances. Off to the side a section of the room had two walls put up and my assumption that it was a small bathroom was correct. The toilet and sink were there along with a stall shower. Next to the bathroom sat a washer and dryer. A little table was off to the side of the kitchen area and a full sized bed. Of course I liked everything I saw but I didn't want to seem eager.

"So what do you think?" she asked leading me to a door that represented a private entrance from the side of the house.

"It's great," I said.

Afterward we discussed rent and I began moving my bags in.

"This is really a nice place you have here," I said as I brought in the last of my things.

"Thank you, we've worked hard on it over the years and I must say that I'm proud of it. My son used to live down here before he finished college and moved away. He's married now with a family of his own. We see them on holidays and special occasions but we usually visit them," she said. "Oh I keep saying "we" but you don't see anyone here but me. My husband is on the road a lot. He owns a little trucking company that keeps him away from home most of the time," she said making her way to the steps leading upstairs. "As you can see you can come and go as you please. I just ask that you don't play your music at a disrespectful level. Here is your key and I hope you enjoy living here. Oh, by the way, my name is Francine. If you need anything just come on up."

"Thanks Francine," I said as I plopped down on my bed. Renting the studio was a great opportunity. It was a blessing from God. I'd never lived on my own and I was looking forward to the solitude. I decided that since I could afford to I'd start looking for a job the following week and spend my first week getting to know Los Angeles and putting some personal touches on my place. I put my new key on my chain, locked up and left.

My goal was to do a little grocery shopping and pick up a few things like a television and portable radio to make my new place feel like home. Driving around I took in all the scenery and noticed all the differences between where I was from and L.A. I could already tell that I just may be in Los Angeles for a while. After making a few stops and asking around I bought some groceries, a TV, radio, and a few things to shine my truck up. The long ride left it looking dull and dirty and it needed to be vacuumed because I'd been eating in it.

When I got back, I put everything away and sat my television on the counter. I placed the radio in the bathroom so I could shower and listen to it, then I grabbed what I needed for my truck and stepped outside to wash it. Just before walking up the last step and being able to be seen from the kitchen window above me, I heard Francine talking to someone. I stopped short because I assumed she was talking about me. I wasn't usually an eavesdropper but I was new in town, had just met the woman, and needed to know who and what I was dealing with.

"Yeah girl, I rented the studio today. Uh-huh and let me tell you that the brotha is fine! Yes, I know and he's young. Mm-mm. Yeah girl I know..." That's all I needed to hear. It was just two women flapping their gums as my dad used to say. I don't know whether it was helpful to know that she was attracted to me, but it sure was interesting.

My mind instantly created a picture that I grinned at then filed away for another time. Right after that I felt something wasn't right with the situation but I couldn't tell what. Deciding it was nothing I pushed what I heard to the back of my mind and continued up the stairs across the yard to my truck on the street.

While opening the driver side door it hit me that I hadn't spoken with my mom in a week. So I made a note to call before going to bed since my family was three hours behind me. I walked back to the house up to the kitchen door and knocked after I pulled out all the products I needed to wash my truck. Before I could ask for what I needed Francine was out the door standing next to me and talking about the water hose.

"Wow," I said, how'd you know I was going to ask for the hose?"

"Well, I saw the bucket and brush and things on the curb so I just figured that's what you needed," she said bending down in front of me to unravel the hose from its hook on the house.

"Oh I've got it," I said bending down next to her to take the hose from her hand. Our hands bumped into each other as she continued to unravel the hose despite me helping. Francine's hands lingered a moment then she pulled them away.

"You know what, this hose probably won't reach to the street and I don't have an extension so you can pull into the driveway to be closer," she said turning and walking toward the door.

"Thanks," I said to her back as the screen door slammed shut. I realized Francine was watching me through the kitchen window but that was okay. I have to say that although her attention was amusing it made me a little uncomfortable because I sensed all kinds of warning signals going off in my mind. They were telling me that I had to keep an eye on her. Yet still learning the voice of the Holy Spirit I pushed those thoughts away and returned to waxing my truck and what I wanted for dinner.

A few days after moving in, Francine's husband Gary returned home from a long distance trip somewhere in Northern California. I immediately liked him because he had a certain way about him that reminded me of my dad plus he was real down to earth and was interesting to talk to. He told me all about his trucking business and how he got started, how many trucks he owned and so forth. After our conversation, I expressed some interest in learning how to drive a tractor trailer, so Gary set things up for me to take driving lessons through a company his business was associated with.

As an incentive he offered me a job if I decided I liked driving big rigs. I told him he had a deal, so I enrolled in the program and about six weeks later I had my CDL. The day I received it Gary was standing outside waiting for me when I got home. I think he was more excited than I was. Even though Gary was old enough to be my dad he treated me like a peer and I both respected and needed that.

"So do I have a new driver or what?" he asked.

"You have a new driver," I said putting my hand out to shake his hand.

"Good. Good," he said pumping my hand then clapped me on the back as we walked inside the house.

"I hear congratulations are in order for both of you," Francine said turning around with a small Carvel cake on a plate.

"I'm looking forward to getting you out on the road and seeing how you fare out there by yourself," Gary said.

"Oh Gary you don't have to send him out long distance so soon, he just started," she said patting my hand then squeezing it for a second. Can't you send him out local for a little while then have him do a long distance run here and there until he gets used to it?" she asked.

"Fran it's all up to James, right James?"

"You know, Francine's right. I think I'll take some local runs for a few weeks to get the hang of it then I'll be ready for wherever you send me."

"Alright, you're the man," he said as we grabbed spoons to eat our ice cream cake.

That night as I lay across my bed reading my Bible I thought about the conversation I had with my family when I got settled in. They couldn't believe I ended up in California. Erica was jealous because she always wanted to see Hollywood, Beverly Hills, and all the other places glamorized on television. My mom as expected was worried about me being so far from home but I assured her I was fine and would call regularly.

Although I'd never been away from home I didn't miss it. I was excited and looking forward to my new life in L.A. I heard a knock at the upstairs door and hurried to put on a tee-shirt on my way to answer it. It was Gary. He told me one of his drivers called out sick so he had to take his load for him and that another driver was scheduled for vacation in a few days and asked if I could take over his loads.

"Sure," I said. "Just let me know the details and I'm on it," I said calmly but on the inside I was ecstatic.

The freedom that came with driving trucks was unparallel with anything I'd ever experienced. That first load turned into several loads then overnight runs then running loads to other states and being gone for days at a time. I loved it. Talking on the CB was an experience I'll never forget. It was like being in your own little community out there on the road.

My handle was "Preacher Man". Some of the drivers from a truck stop a lot of us frequented started calling me that name when they saw me blessing my food and reading my Bible. After a while, I got up the nerve to witness. I'm not ashamed of God and His message, but there's something about conversations regarding politics and spiritual beliefs. I heard once that you don't have to know the Bible inside and out to be a good witness, you just have to show up willing to put yourself out there and the Holy Spirit will do the rest.

Afterwards, the Holy Spirit will tell you what needs to be said in order to touch people. We have to share the good news, because there are people in hell right now wishing that family members, co-workers, neighbors, and anyone else they came in contact with that knew the Gospel shared it with them. But it's too late and I can imagine them wondering why they didn't share it.

I know why though… well, I know why I didn't want to at first. It's because I didn't want to be rejected and I didn't want to be challenged over what I believe. I was totally surprised when I learned my dad received Jesus, but I know in my heart that I would've never spoken a word to him about salvation because I was afraid of what he might say to me or how he might view me. Sometimes I wonder whether I would've said something to him on his death bed. Thank God someone that knew who he was in Christ witnessed to him. My dad might be in hell today waiting for me to get up the nerve.

Despite my fear, after hearing sermon after sermon something inside me broke and I was able to shake off the timidity and uncertainty of the strength of my testimony. I hadn't been delivered from drugs, alcohol, prison, or anything impressive like that and I wondered who would care about what God had done in my life, but all I had to do was be willing and the Holy Spirit did the rest. In the first two months of driving trucks and frequenting that particular truck stop, five people got saved and another rededicated his life. I didn't mind being called Preacher Man.

❧

Before I knew it a year passed that I'd been working for Gary and living in his basement. One day when I was outside changing the oil on my truck Gary kneeled down and asked me to come from under it. When I did, he had a serious look on his face and I wondered what was wrong so I asked.

"Nothing's wrong man. I just want to know if you'd like a promotion."

"A promotion? What kind of promotion can I get as a driver? I already get lots of overtime and first pick of the runs I make," I said laughing.

"No, I mean a promotion from driving to being in charge of the drivers. You said you went to junior college for business so why don't you apply what you learned here," he said spreading his arms.

"What about dispatch?" I asked.

"You'll be over them as well," he said.

The thought had crossed my mind a few times that running a trucking business seemed relatively easy and appealed to me but I never thought about running Gary's.

"I have to think about it. I mean I don't have any experience other than from a driver's perspective," I said.

"Well, with the mind you have plus your driving experience I believe you can keep the company running and the drivers and customers happy," he said holding his hand out for a handshake to seal the deal.

"Alright, I'll do my best," I said giving his hand a firm shake. Afterward Gary dusted himself off and turned to leave. My heart raced as I slid back under the truck. Little by little I somehow elevated from tenant to a live-in family friend that paid rent. It was a little awkward at first when Gary and Francine invited me to have dinner one night because Gary wanted to talk about my runs. The next thing I knew one night here and there when Gary was home turned into a few nights a week if Gary was away and if Francine wasn't busy, to eating dinner every evening with both of them, one of them, or by myself because Francine left me a plate. It got to the place where I hardly bothered buying any groceries beyond toiletries and snacks.

One night when Gary was home we watched a couple of movies and the next thing I knew I woke up on the couch I was sitting on with a blanket over me. I got up and folded the blanket and went to my basement apartment where I belonged. I felt things were becoming too familiar between us so I decided to do something about it. What that something was I didn't know because I didn't want to offend them. By the time Gary decided to promote me I still hadn't figured out how to pull away from him, but with the promotion how could I pull myself away? Not only that, but Gary wanted to know that whoever ran his business was trustworthy. I'm not stupid. Although I could tell Gary and Francine genuinely liked me, I perceived a few tests here and there but I didn't mind them.

The smart thing for me to do at that time was to continue in the direction we were moving. I made the decision to let them have control of the flow of our relationship because I knew things would continue to run smoothly for me. Although we were friends I was still a tenant and an employee and had to continue to maintain a certain level of trust with them.

About two weeks later I began my new role in Gary's company. It was interesting to see the responses I received from the drivers I used to run with after Gary announced my promotion. I knew a few guys talked about having a position similar to mine but they never pursued it. Some of them stopped talking to me because they saw me as being different but I didn't change. Their opinion of me changed. There were others who congratulated me and encouraged me, so I was able to determine who was a friend and who wasn't.

After being in the office for a month and a half I solved a time management issue that saved Gary some money. In addition to that, I was able to work out a contract between Gary's company and Le Bol Corporation whom Gary had never been successful in winning as a client. I knew I had God's favor flowing in my life. It seemed like everything I put my hands to succeeded. If there was a problem I was able to figure it out. Now by no means am I a simple man but I also know myself. I wouldn't have been able to come up with the answers to the issues that kept popping up. God was with me and His Holy Spirit was speaking to me and teaching me.

Chapter 6

James

Lord, You shared a mystery and gave me the key…

I was fortunate to find a good church in Inglewood that I attended regularly, and after inviting them Francine and Gary made it out a few times. One Sunday, one of the ministers spoke on the favor of God and how people, even those that don't go to church can tell that you're blessed. He said they'll want to be apart of whatever you're apart of because they know it's blessed. It doesn't matter if they're a believer or not, God will bless them for helping you.

A month after hearing that message I had a dream about three huge barrels that stood several stories high. The barrels were the height of city buildings. Everyone around me drove up to the barrels in their cars and trucks and tractor trailers and got out. They started beating on the barrels in anger. I didn't understand what was going on as I stood and watched the chaos. People were running everywhere and grabbing their hair in handfuls. When I reached one of the barrels some of whatever was in it splashed to the ground before me and I bent down and put a finger in the puddle and smelled it. It was fuel. When I woke up I realized I dreamt about something but I couldn't put all the pieces together to make any sense of it.

Later that day at the office while I was eating lunch and reading the paper I stopped chewing as my eyes focused on the word *fuel*. My dream was immediately brought back to me and I instantly understood the meaning of it. The people were running around in anguish because of the fuel. The fuel was in barrels that were huge and full to the brim but no one could access it. I knew in my heart that the fuel was expensive and that the price of fuel would greatly increase sometime in the future.

The increase in price would last for three months hence there being three barrels. I didn't know how to take that dream. I'd always dreamed but not this vividly and I never felt that I knew the meaning of them until the dream about the barrels. That night I thanked God for the meaning of the interesting dream because I believed it was a message from Him.

That night I dreamed about the barrels again and I put my finger in the fuel just like before. It was the exact same dream. By that point I was interested, curious, and a little afraid so immediately after the dream I got out of bed and onto my knees because fuel was an important resource that the trucking industry depended on. If fuel became too expensive to purchase Gary's company would go under along with many others. I prayed and asked God what could be done because He didn't have to share that information with me. That meant He was warning me and telling me to be prepared.

"But Father how do I prepare?" I cried out in the middle of the night. "What do I do? What do I do? What can *I* do? Please help me. Give me the wisdom and knowledge that I need to help Gary's business succeed," I prayed over and over. I got back into bed expecting God to reveal the answer to me that night but my alarm clock went off without me dreaming anything else. I was a little upset because I wanted to get a move on whatever I could do.

Every night for a week, I went to bed after seeking God and even questioned whether He gave me the dream in the first place until one day while sitting at my desk it came to me. God gave me the solution. I came up with the idea to cut corners in different areas of the business that I hadn't thought of before. In addition, I was able to increase the amount of money banked from weekly profits made. No one, not even Gary noticed the little changes that were made or even the fact that the business was being run on less money than usual. That was supernatural.

I didn't know exactly when the price of fuel would increase but I felt that it was a ways off- less than a year away but more than six months. So we saved and saved operating on less but maintaining. This took place for eight months, our money saved increasing, then one day just before the eighth month ended, I heard the Holy Spirit tell me to get ready.

"Get ready for what Lord?" I asked truly not realizing what He was talking about.

"Get ready," He said again and my thoughts turned to what I'd been preparing for. In a few days time Gary burst into the building startling the receptionist talking about how he can't believe the price of fuel was going up.

"I don't believe this!" he yelled. "How do they expect us to make it paying so much for fuel?! What about us?!"

"What's going on?" I asked knowing full well that I was anticipating the moment.

"Read this," he groaned shoving a newspaper into my hand. It said gas prices were set to soar and no end to the price hike could be foreseen.

"Gary calm down," I said knowing I'd react the same way if I hadn't gotten a heads up from God.

"Listen, I've been preparing for this. Carvey Distribution is going to be fine. You'll see," I said reassuring him.

"What do you mean you've been preparing for this?" he asked looking at me like I had three heads.

"I knew this was going to happen because God showed me in a dream several months ago."

"You mean to tell me that you had a dream and you actually believed it? Whenever I dream I'm running from something, looking for something, or don't even remember that I dreamt. Honestly, I don't even remember the last time I had a dream."

"Well, I've always dreamed but I didn't always remember them. But the ones I remembered I wrote down. Now I can tell the difference between which ones are just dreams and when God is talking to me. At first I wasn't sure about this particular dream but when I dreamt it two nights in a row I knew God was trying to tell me something," I said proud of the fact that God used me to save Gary's company and the families represented there.

I told Gary all about the dream and how God showed me what to do to prepare for the increase in fuel. Gary looked at me in amazement then hugged me.

"Hallelujah!" he yelled and laughed out loud as he waved his hands in the air in a fake praise. He didn't even check the accounts or ask me what it was that I did. He just took my word for it and strolled confidently to his office. At the end of the day Gary walked over to my desk and sat down on the edge.

"I checked the accounts a few minutes ago," he said. "I don't know how you and God did it but you managed to save more money than I've ever been able to save during some of my busiest seasons."

"Well God did it all," I said. "He just used me to do it."

"You just keep on doing what you do to keep the money rolling in and things running smoothly around here," he said holding his hand out for five. I gave him five and shook my head at his excitement and leaned my chair back on its back legs to savor the moment.

That evening all the news channels were broadcasting live at gas stations and speaking with angry or fearful customers regarding their thoughts on the price hike. People were yelling into the microphones and were so emotional about the situation that the reporters had to snatch their mics from their hands to gain control. Sitting there watching the news I thought about God's goodness and offered up a prayer of thanks.

"Thank you Heavenly Father for speaking to me and using me to save Carvey Distribution. I don't know why You chose me or why You even take time to think of me, but you guide my steps and take care of me every step of the way. Thank you Lord for the supernatural impartation of wisdom and I pray that as I continue to listen for your Holy Spirit that I continue to easily and clearly hear Him and quickly obey. Thank you Father God for Your unconditional love. In the name of Jesus I pray. Amen."

With that I got up and pushed my chair under my desk and left the building. Within the next few weeks things turned really bad for others. People were going to jail for trying to steal gas and police officers were posted at gas stations all over. We, on the other hand were walking around conducting business like nothing was happening. It felt good to be walking in God's favor.

The following week our receptionist transferred a call to my desk in Gary's absence. It was Bill Talley, the owner of our biggest competitor, Diesel Trucking. He asked to speak with Gary in a curt manner but I responded politely that he wasn't in the office and that I could help him.

"What did you say your name is?"

"James Anderson."

"James what? Aren't you the boy Gary hired to drive for him not too long ago and you live in his basement?"

"Yes, I'm an employee here and I'm renting his basement."

"Hmm, and what was it you said your position is now?" he asked.

"I'm the...,"

"I need to speak with Gary not you," he said cutting me off. "I need to speak with someone who can make sound decisions around there. Talk business. Not some little ambitious punk that's barely beyond puberty."

"Well sir, I'm sorry you feel that way but Gary discusses all his business decisions with me before he proceeds with anything regarding Carvey Distribution. Not only does he discuss business with me but he goes with whatever decision I make," I said arrogantly.

"Oh my goodness! You've got to be kidding me! This fuel thing must be getting to Gary's head. When will he be back?" he asked.

"Gary will be back in the office tomorrow morning," I said.

"Click." He hung up on me. That wasn't the first time someone didn't care for the fact that I was in charge of so much at Gary's company, yet so young.

The next morning when Gary walked into the office he walked straight to my desk and sat on the edge of it. I was on the phone and he stayed there until my call ended.

"I need to speak with you about something important," he said still sitting on my desk.

"Okay," I responded slowly.

"How would you like to officially be second in charge of Carvey Distribution? Everyone that has anything to do with Carvey Distribution will answer to you. You'll make all the decisions around here with my authority behind everything you decide to do. You've got a special connection to the man upstairs," he said pointing up, "and ever since you came here everything's worked out for me. I know that with you running Carvey Distribution we'll be the biggest thing on the West coast," he said almost of breath.

"Of course," I said standing up to shake Gary's hand.

"Good. Good. First thing tomorrow morning, I want you to get started with the new addition to the building."

"New addition?" I questioned.

"Yeah, your new office. My second in command can't be sitting at a raggedy desk in the corner of a room," he said slapping me on the back and laughing. Smiling I shook my head in amazement and sat down behind my desk. Although we hadn't discussed a salary increase I knew there would be one. That meant I could afford to move out of Gary's basement and not touch the money from dad's insurance policy.

I was elated about having my own office and immediately pulled out a phone book to look for contractors to provide an estimate for the addition to the building. With that done I flipped through the pages until I found the real estate section. My days of living in Gary and Francine's basement were over.

"James," Gary said interrupting my thoughts. "I hope you don't have any plans tonight because Francine and I would like to take you to dinner to celebrate."

"Um, sure. I look forward to it," I said making a mental change of plans from checking out realtors to eating with them. Gary hired a driver to take the three of us to Seth's, the most expensive restaurant in L.A. I was thoroughly impressed. We ordered appetizers and Francine and Gary ordered a bottle of the most expensive champagne at Seth's restaurant. When the waiter attempted to pour champagne in my glass I told him no thanks but Gary insisted. I settled with the fact that Gary could insist on the champagne being in my glass but he couldn't make me drink it.

"To the new addition to Carvey Distribution and many years of success," Gary said.

"Here. Here."

"And to new friends and relationships," Francine quickly added."

"Here. Here."

The three of us held up our glasses, Gary and Francine with their champagne and me with a glass of water.

"James, you're not going to join us and have a glass of champagne?" Francine prodded.

"I've never been much of a drinker," I lied. "It gives me headaches that last for days. Besides I need to be alert to run Carvey Distribution," I laughed. Gary and Francine laughed too.

"Well I certainly don't want anything keeping you from making decisions," Gary chuckled.

In the middle of dinner and a few beers later Gary excused himself to the restroom.

"So how does it feel to be in charge of your own company James?"

I chuckled then said, "Well, you know Carvey Distribution isn't my company but it feels good, real good holding a high position and being Gary's right hand man."

"You wear it well for such a young man. The pressure and the stress don't get to you?"

"Of course there are days that I'm faced with tough decisions but those are the times I rely heaviest on my Father," I said pointing up.

"Yes, I know what you mean," she said then paused as if thinking of how to word what she wanted to say next. "I've never seen you bring a young woman home and you seem to hardly go out except for the gym, groceries, church, and work. Is your schedule getting in the way of your social life?" she inquired with an admiring look.

"Right now I'm not looking for anyone. I'm concentrating on where God is leading me with the business. I trust that when that time comes He'll bring the right woman into my life at the right time."

"You're really something, you know that? You're waiting for God to bring the right woman into your life. Hmph. You don't need God to help you do that because from the looks of things in here there are plenty of women you can have your pick of."

Feeling myself blush and hating that I allowed Francine to see it , I quickly changed the subject.

"Where did you say your son lives again?"

"Oh come on, you can do way better than that to get me off the subject," she laughed with a gleam in her eye. "Now back to what we were talking about. There are a lot of women in here that would pay for a moment of your time and here I am sitting across from you," she said shifting herself in her chair. "I want you to know that I'm a fan too," she said caressing my hand and licking her lips. "And you know what I mean."

I snatched my hand away just before Gary strolled back to the table. My heart pumping, I excused myself to the restroom and stood in a stall. I couldn't believe what Francine said and did in public right behind Gary's back. To make matters worse I was aroused by it. "Lord, help me," I prayed as I looked up. "Please help me to get through this dinner and out of Gary's house. Forgive me God," I said as I tightened my tie then adjusted my pants.

Throughout the rest of dinner, I could hardly keep track of the conversation thinking about how Francine acted when Gary was in the bathroom. I wondered if that was normal behavior for her. The ride back home was quiet. I sat on one side and Gary was asleep with his head on Francine's lap on the other. Every now and then I caught Francine looking at me from the corner of my eye but I didn't acknowledge it. I didn't want to throw fuel on anymore advances from her especially in the presence of Gary. Minutes before arriving home Francine woke Gary and the two of them stumbled to the front door as I entered my apartment below through the side entrance.

After loosening my tie, I felt a tremendous urge to pray. I threw off my suit jacket and undid the first few buttons of my shirt. I was so troubled. I couldn't understand why in the midst of such a happy time for me that I was feeling like this. I should've been on cloud nine. But there was something going on that I needed to pray about. I was overcome with a desire to pray. I fell to my knees at the couch before reaching my usual spot on the bed.

"Oh God, what is it Father?" I really didn't know where to begin so

I just started thanking Him. "O thank You Father. Hallelujah. Praise Your name Father God. You're an awesome God. You're an on time God. You are my source! You are my strength. You are my everything. You give me favor among men God. You're my deliverer." Then I began to pray for different family members but the feeling was still there. I even prayed for those that were struggling to pay for fuel. I thanked Him for my budding career and then I prayed for Francine and Gary. Lord knows Francine needed prayer, however I felt I could handle her.

At that time my lips and tongue waved with the flow of my Heavenly prayer language. It flowed and flowed and tears streamed down my face. I didn't understand why the Holy Spirit wanted me to pray for Francine and Gary. I knew they weren't saved and I even invited them to church but it seemed like there was more going on. Even more than their obvious marital problems. I ended my prayer in Jesus' name and pushed myself to my feet to finish undressing and get ready for bed. Lying in bed I thought about my new position, the trust Gary had in me, and my new office. Even more so I contemplated where I wanted to move because I absolutely couldn't continue living under Gary's roof.

Over the next few months, Carvey Distribution, or CarDi as I like to call it experienced supernatural increase. The day to day business became so busy that I had to push my plans of looking for my own home aside so I could keep up with things. I did however get the ball rolling with the addition to the building. Not only would I be gaining a new more spacious office but a conference area and new employee lounge were going to be added as well. I couldn't forget the other employees.

Around the time I signed the contract for new construction I received another call from Bill Talley, the owner of Diesel Trucking. Once again he was rude but it was toned down a bit.

"Look, I want some kind of partnership with Carvey Distribution," Mr. Talley said.

"That's impossible Mr. Talley. We're not partnering with Diesel Trucking no matter what, plain and simple. I have big plans for this company that don't include stepping beneath ourselves by joining with you," I said.

"Who do you think you are, talking to me like that young man? I'll put in calls and have you out on your behind. I'll…"

"You'll do nothing but shut up and talk to Tone."

"Who? What?…," was all I heard him saying as I hung up to give him time with Tone- the dial tone. I didn't have time for his foolishness and nonsense. He would never agree to a partnership if the tables were turned. I laughed quietly at myself remembering what I said to him before hanging up, then I got up from my desk and told the receptionist that I'd be gone for a few hours.

I'd done some calling around to check on the status of several trucking companies and all of them were losing business due to the cost of fuel. One of my goals was to acquire more trucks for the company. Not just tractor trailers but dump trucks, delivery trucks, and whatever else was for sale and in good shape. I drove an hour to one trucking company that had two black MAC trucks for sale. I pulled into the parking lot, said a prayer, and got out walking toward the trucks. I hopped up onto the step of one of them to peek into the window on the driver's side. The exterior was in good condition and the interior seemed to be intact as well. The stickers on the truck were up to date and everything looked good. I did the same check on the other truck then asked the owner for the keys to take a better look inside the cabs.

The floors were clean. The dash was wiped down and shining in both trucks. The mats were clean and in place and everything looked perfect. I started both trucks and just sat there listening to the roar of the engine. I entered the building and said, "Let's talk some numbers." Thirty minutes later I cut a business check purchasing the two trucks. I gathered the envelopes containing all the information I needed for the trucks and headed home. I decided the next time I went out I'd have drivers follow me so the trucks could be delivered to Carvey Distribution the same day.

Every week, I purchased more trucks one after the other. We acquired so many trucks that we had to rent out the empty lot next to our building to park them. Then as if on cue men and women began calling for jobs. I hadn't even put ads in the paper yet because the trucks had to be registered to the company, receive new tags, get new paint jobs, and get new lettering.

Potential employees were on a waiting list. Soon, we had to hire another dispatcher and instead of contacting mechanics to service our trucks they were contacting us. Fifty paint jobs later there were rows and rows of tractor trailers sporting the company name of Carvey Distribution. I was proud of the empire God was using me to grow for Gary. So much had gone on since fuel prices went up but only two months had passed. The Holy Spirit let me know that there was one month left and that I had a lot of work to do before the prices returned to normal.

We ended up buying the one story building we were renting including the large lot beside it. We had plans in order to build a huge garage to house the trucks as well as a servicing area in the rear. Before long Carvey Distribution trucks were seen all over the roads. We were getting so much work that we almost didn't have enough drivers. I had a secretary and a personal assistant as did Gary although I was doing all the work.

Francine took her place as queen of the empire visiting the building often and hiring a decorating firm. One thing about Francine is that she wasn't polite to people all of a sudden. She waltzed into the building in high-heeled shoes, form fitting ensembles, and practically threw her coat and purse at the receptionist after entering. Afterward she'd stand in the lobby for a moment as if waiting for someone to announce that she'd arrived. She ordered things be brought to her instead of asking and had everyone except me on pins and needles when she was there.

"And how are we doing today?" She asked me one day, after entering my office unannounced. I was relaxing on my ultra plush sofa after a long conference call then quickly sat up to straighten my tie and tuck my shirt into my pants.

"I'm fine Francine. Is there something I can help you with?" I asked obviously annoyed as I stepped into my shoes.

"I just stopped by to see how you're doing. To see how the famous James Anderson keeps making me richer and richer," she said approaching me stopping only inches from my face. Just as she raised a hand to touch my cheek there was a knock at the door.

"Mr. Anderson?" I heard my secretary say. I hurried to the door to get away from Francine and opened it wide. "These packages are for you. My desk is already stacked so I figured you wouldn't mind if I dropped them off in your office."

"Oh sure. No problem. I realize you've been bogged down with all the work I've been giving you. As a matter of fact, its three o'clock now, you can leave for the day as soon as you get your things together."

"Thank you Mr. Anderson," she blushed and walked down the hall.

"I see you have an admirer here," Francine said walking toward my couch to perch herself seductively across it.

"Francine if there's nothing you need me to do for you could you please leave?" I asked raising my voice a little.

"Oh you know what you can do for me," she said boldly lifting her leg to allow her thigh to show through the daringly high split.

"Please get out!" I said through clenched teeth as I hurried over to where she was. I must have scared her a little because she jumped up before I reached her. I took her by the upper arm and practically pushed her toward the door.

"You may not think so right now but I'm going to have you. Either you give me what I want or I'll take what you want," she spat at me.

"You can't take anything from me because you haven't given anything to me. The only thing I'm going to give you is some advice. Stay away from me and get some help because whatever you have planned ain't gonna happen. You think you can walk into my office acting like you're not married to my boss then try to force me into doing what you want?! Get out!" I said pushing her into the hall and locking my office door. Francine was a trip and was becoming a huge problem.

Just then the receptionist buzzed me. "Mr. Anderson, David Williams from the L.A. Gazette is on line one for you," she said excitedly.

"Thank you Ashley." Wondering what the call was about I quickly cleared my throat and took the call. "Mr. Williams, how are you?"

"Oh, I'm great sir but I'll be even better if I can get an interview with you. My sources tell me that Carvey Distribution is growing by leaps and bounds and is destroying the competition."

"Well, you do know that I'm not the owner of this company but..."

"But you're the one who makes all the decisions. My sources also tell me that Carvey Distribution would be nothing without you. As a matter of fact they say that although you make a handsome salary you're grossly under paid for all that you do. What do you have to say about that?"

"First of all are you calling to ask if I'll do the interview or to give the interview? I'm not answering any questions until I've agreed to the interview," I responded.

"Oh, my apologies sir, I'm just so thrilled to be speaking to the man who is single handedly rebuilding a company that was nowhere near as successful just a few short months ago. I want to have a sit down and get to know the real James Anderson and share what I've learned with everyone else. When can we meet?"

"I'll have to transfer you to my secretary Bernice and she'll be able to set things up." "Okay then Mr. Anderson, we'll be meeting soon. Have a good day."

"Same to you."

After receiving the reporter's call something inside me began to churn. I was excited because all my efforts to transform Carvey Distribution into a successful business were paying off and getting attention. I mean Carvey Distribution was getting well deserved attention.

At the end of the day, I stopped by Gary's office. When he saw me peek my head into the room he looked up and said, "Just the man I was to see. Sit down for a moment."

"Sure boss. What's on your mind?"

"I'm planning to take Francine on a trip for about two weeks then after that I'll be gone for a week to attend the convention I was telling you about. I know you said you didn't mind going but we need you here doing the important stuff."

"Gary I was going to tell you this tomorrow but since we're here now I might as well tell you. I was asked to be interviewed by David Williams from the L.A. Gazette," I said pretty sure Gary would be excited.

"Ah man, we're being interviewed! That's great news man! I can't believe this! We are really gonna be on top! When's the interview?"

"I don't know. I told him to set something up with Bernice. I'm going to check right now if you don't mind."

"Sure, use my phone." I stood up and bent over Gary's desk to buzz my secretary.

"Hey Bernice, I'm in Gary's office. Can you tell me what day you scheduled the interview for?"

"Yes. Next Tuesday, the twelfth. Your whole afternoon is free so I scheduled it for one o'clock. He's treating you to lunch at Daphne's. The article will appear on the front page of the paper."

"Thanks Bernice. Good job."

"Man, I won't be here," Gary said. "We're leaving early Sunday morning for the Virgin Islands. Francine deserves it. She's a good wife. She keeps the house and pays the bills while I'm away. She keeps me in line and the things she's doing around here with decorating are great don't you think?"

"Uh, yuh-yeah. She's doing a great job. Everyone talks about how nice everything is in here since we remodeled."

"She's my heart," he said leaning back in his plush chair with his hands behind his head. Looking at him in pity and disbelief I said goodbye and excused myself from his office.

❧

The day of the interview I drove to Daphne's although I could've had the company limo take me. I left at noon knowing there would be more volume on the highways due to lunchtime, and made perfect time. I didn't know what to expect when I entered the restaurant so I prayed on my way there that God would give me what to say should I be asked a question I didn't know the answer to, or didn't want to answer.

Reaching the reporter's table I extended my hand and took a seat. We placed our orders and the interview began immediately after our waitress left. The questions weren't prying or annoying at all. I was asked questions about my background, the company, the success of the company, and my hopes for the future of the company. When asked about the key to my success I gave honor where all honor is due. I told him that it wasn't me. It was all God. I could tell that he was a little disappointed with my response, until I explained my dream. After that he seemed to become more interested. About an hour later we stood up, shook hands and went our separate ways.

A few days later Ashley stopped by my office with an armload of papers. She pointed to the article and grinned as she placed two papers on my desk. Apparently my perception of Dave's opinion of me was wrong. He wrote an eloquent article about a young man from New Jersey with ambition and a special connection to "the man upstairs" that single handedly turned a company that was mediocre at best into one of the leading trucking companies in the state of California. I smiled as I read and re-read the article, then asked Ashley to overnight a paper to my mom.

I talked to my mom about everything going on, even Francine. She once told me that she'd get on a plane and "knock Francine upside her head" if she didn't keep her claws off me. She said it jokingly but I knew there was a little bit of truth in it because mama don't play when it comes to her kids.

The next thing I knew I started getting calls left and right from *Trucker's Weekly, Keep On Trucking, and Tractor Trailers*, to name a few. Everyone wanted a chance to interview me to find out my secret to success during a time when everyone else was struggling with the decision to buy gas versus other necessities. Before I knew it I was out of the office more than I was in because of people wanting to take me to lunch and would you believe it- to touch me! I guess they thought my favor would rub off on them – literally!

The attention I was getting made me feel different. It made me feel both important and excited. My life was exciting. I felt like a celebrity because people outside of the trucking industry were starting to notice me. It got to the point where when I went to the grocery store people recognized me and even asked me for my autograph! Women of all ages, shapes, sizes, races, and backgrounds gravitated to me giving me their phone numbers on pieces of paper, business cards, yelling them out from passing cars, and even buying me drinks when I dined out. My mom warned me about these things when I sent her the newspaper and I assured her that I could handle everything with God in my corner.

However, as bold as I was in saying that, I became so busy with maintaining the business and growing the company that my relationship with God took a backseat. My prayers in the morning after reading my Bible became a quick "Good morning Father" to no Bible at all and my prayers forgotten. I used to pray in the middle of the day whenever I wanted to because I could. Eventually those prayer times were pushed away and forgotten because of business meetings, conference room brainstorming, and well, thinking of ways more money could be made. I was on top when it came to my career but my relationship with God wasn't what it used to be. Francine was relentless. At one time, I prayed for her and Gary but because my prayer life was dying I saw no change.

I eventually moved out and into my own home like I planned to. There was a warehouse that had space to purchase and different floors had already been renovated into condos, so I jumped on the opportunity. I bought a new truck and a sports car and donated my old truck to charity. I was making money because I was making Gary so much money. As Gary's right hand man he was lead around by everything I said and decided was best for CarDi. I was like God to him. Like God?

At some point there was a shift in everything and if I was vigilant and being careful I would've noticed and checked myself. However, the fact that I reached that point meant that something was already wrong. I'm sure the Holy Spirit was trying to speak to me. But because I was busy making money I couldn't hear what He was saying, nor did I desire to really listen. Since I barely had a prayer life anymore I wasn't praying in my Heavenly prayer language and didn't even notice until it was too late that I wasn't hearing the voice of the Holy Spirit as easily and clearly as I used to.

Despite realizing this I didn't handle the situation the way I should've. In fact I didn't handle it at all. Before leaving Jersey, I was attending both Sunday and Wednesday services and serving in different ministries at the church. After finding a church in L.A. I found my place and picked up where I left off in Jersey. Now, I was still tithing and giving offering but my absences from church were piling up and people other than myself were beginning to notice. I realized this truth one evening as I relaxed on my Italian leather sofa sipping a glass of white wine.

The phone rang and it was a woman from the Angel in My Corner ministry at the church. She was calling because it came to the pastor's attention that I'd missed five Sunday services within the past two months and the last two were back to back. I was angry after that call, and started pacing around my den. Saved and filled with the Holy Spirit or not, I've never liked being checked on and asked why or why not I'm doing something. The next thing I knew I cursed as some of the wine I was drinking splashed from the glass onto the gleaming hardwood floor I had been stomping back and forth on.

"Who do they think they are checking up on me? Do they realize I'm a grown man and that I don't need them or anyone else checking up on me? I work hard all week long and those weeks I even went in on Saturday so I skipped church to get some rest," I said to no one in particular- at least I thought, because God was listening to my tirade. "Mom hasn't even had to touch the money Dad left her because I would send her and Erica money every month. My step-pop calls all the time telling me what they're doing to the house, what they're adding on, or what they're going to purchase. That's because of my hard work and now I'm getting calls from church because I haven't been there in a few Sundays! They know how hard I work. I got several of them jobs with CarDi and they have the nerve to be checking up on me. I don't hear anyone complaining about the new heating and cooling system I had installed at the church as soon as I found out there was a problem. Naw, James don't like being checked up on like some kid. I'ma grown man!" I immediately made up in my mind that I wasn't going to church that upcoming Sunday either as if my not being there was punishing the church.

By that time several months had passed and CarDi was becoming an empire. We bought some land and had real estate built on it because we needed a second location. We hired more drivers to operate all the new trucks we purchased from dealers but mainly from owners who could no longer afford them as well as two new dispatchers.

Gary and Francine put their house up for sale and moved into a ritzy development. It suited Francine. However, Gary seemed out of place but ecstatic at all he had achieved, I mean all I achieved for him. My mind began to wonder what it would be like if CarDi were mine. Honestly, it already seemed like it was. Gazing out of my ceiling to floor view that traveled the entire length of the western side of my condo I looked out at the city, the homes, and the sky, as the sun set and I imagined owning all of it, having the power to manipulate it all if given the chance. Almost satisfied with what I'd accomplished for myself in such a short period of time, my chest puffed up and I exhaled in pride.

That night after getting into bed I sat up and pulled the covers over my lap and pulled my Bible and evening devotional from my nightstand. I read the devotional dated for that day and read a random chapter from the Old Testament half comprehending what it was saying to me. Clicking the lamp off, I slid further under the covers and turned onto my left side going over the day's events. I felt the weird feeling that goes along with knowing you should pray but not knowing what to pray about and even more so not even feeling like praying.

I didn't feel that familiar and soothing desire to just lay there and talk to God about whatever, such as my day, my life, just things on my mind and close to my heart like I used to. I liked those times because it was as if God was sitting in my room on the edge of my bed or the easy chair in the corner of my room waiting for us to talk like two old friends. I closed my eyes but my mind wouldn't rest. I don't know how long I laid there before I finally fell asleep.

At breakfast the next morning my housekeeper hummed as she moved around my kitchen clinking dishes, pans, and silverware while she tidied up after preparing my meal. Looking off in a daze after eating, my mind visited a place I'd been just several months ago. I saw in my mind's eye the happiness I felt after having two or three dreams back to back, knowing they were from God and knowing what they meant. God hadn't been speaking to me in the night at all lately and it bothered me. In the back of my mind I thought about changing some things around in my life so I could get back the relationship I used to have and…

"Mr. Anderson, Mr. Anderson, you okay? The phone, it's for you," my housekeeper said wrinkling her brow and handing me the phone.

I came out of my day dream and took the call. It was Denise reminding me about a ten o'clock meeting that I absolutely couldn't cancel. "Thanks Denise. See you in an hour," I said hanging up the phone.

ભ

"Yes, yes, exactly, Carvey Distribution will be honored to serve you," I said to a new client I just sealed a deal with. "Alright, I'm going to transfer you to my assistant and she'll forward you the documents for your signature. We look forward to working with you Sir. Goodbye."

It was funny to me how my life was changing and I seemed to have no control over it. I thought about my career, my family, my plans for the future, God, and everything else. My life. Never before consumed by such thoughts I felt myself becoming depressed, and instead of turning to God because all of my help comes from Him, I turned to my own devices. In the process I developed a little dependency on alcohol to relax me after a long day, which became everyday, and to celebrate new clients, to compliment my dinner and, well, whenever I felt like it. Not only that, but Francine slipped her way into my plans many times, stopping by my place to break the marriage vows she never cared anything about anyway.

At first I was ashamed of what we were doing, but eventually I felt a strange sense of entitlement somehow. After all, the new house, car, clothes, and other things she had were because of me. After several times I just plain didn't care. She had the nerve to try to keep me pinned down too, as if she was the only woman after me. Please. I had so many women after me it was ridiculous.

Then things began to get a little complicated. Out of nowhere Francine started sending me letters threatening to disclose our relationship if I didn't continue seeing her. I chuckled a bit when I received the first few letters but after a month passed the situation got a little more serious. Her threatening letters were no longer scented with some type of perfume trying to draw me in.

In their place were tape recordings of conversations we'd had about Gary in which I was completely drunk at the time, slurring my words and joking about our secret. When I finally confronted Francine about what she was doing and reiterated that we couldn't keep seeing each other, she cursed me and said I'd regret it and hung up on me. Instead of Francine getting a grip on reality and realizing that it was best for the two us to stop while we were ahead, she decided to get ugly, and I mean butt ugly.

As I usually do, one evening after work I sat down in my den to open my mail. I went through the pile tossing envelope after envelope of credit card offers and invitations to this one's little get together and that one's little fundraising event, then an envelope that I somehow overlooked fell to the floor. There was no return address but the postage markings on it showed that it came from somewhere in L.A., and I vaguely recognized the handwriting.

After I opened the envelope, I saw a small corner of a photo inside. I was sure that the contractor I hired to remodel the lobby of one of our offices sent pictures of his progress. However, when I pulled the rest of the photos out, my mouth flew open in horror and I jumped up so quickly I almost knocked over my couch. I could not believe my eyes.

Francine had absolutely lost it. I mean she was completely out of it to do what she did. Inside that envelope wasn't one, but ten different photos of Francine and I together in my condo, and we weren't talking business. I immediately scrambled to the phone to call Francine and ask her what in the world she was thinking, and who in the world she had taking photos of us, but I caught myself figuring that response would only set her off even more. In the back of my mind I saw flashbacks of me prior to the mess I found myself in. I wanted to go back there and not have to deal with whatever situation Francine was trying to create. The entitlement I felt just moments before opening the envelope slowly turned to guilt.

Instead I took a few deep breaths to clear my head, and once my pulse stopped raging I dialed her number. I knew Gary wouldn't be there because he was handling some business that he decided to do on his own for once, so Francine and I could speak freely over the phone. I couldn't wait to find out why she was trying to ruin my career and her marriage for a silly relationship that was based on nothing but sex, adulterous sex at that.

"Hello Francine?!" I asked in an enraged voice when she answered the phone.

"Yes, who's this?" She asked knowing darn well it was me.

"You know exactly who this is and you better stop playing these games and get yourself together!" I yelled! I forgot about upsetting her and making things worse.

"James are you so confident in yourself that you think you can outwit me or talk me into doing something I don't want to do like some of your clients? You're not gonna use me and then put me out on the curb like I'm trash."

"Hey, I'm not the one who came after you relentlessly. You threatened my career if I didn't comply to your demands. You are the one cheating on your husband. So if that sounds like trash to you, then you said it, not me."

Francine with fire in her voice replied, "Oh, you think you're so smart. Well, we'll see how smart you think you are after I do what I've got planned next. You're going to do exactly as I say or else I'm going to ruin you, James Anderson. You're gonna wish you'd just gone along with the program like the others before you."

"You know what, I..." I said then decided I should let Francine have the last word and deal with her on another day. "Can we talk about this tomorrow?" I asked allowing her to think that her will was stronger than mine.

"That's more like it," she said in a victorious voice. "I knew you'd begin seeing things my way."

"Sure, whatever you say," I told her just before she hung up. I fell back on my couch exasperated wondering how my life had come to this after having an intimate relationship with God. I had done more than backslidden. I took some serious steps backward spiritually and considered the consequences. I didn't want to pay by losing anything. Not my career. Not anything.

✌

Despite my problems with the boss's wife, everything else was flowing smoothly. Business was going even better with the purchase of a gas station on a main highway that many people frequented. We enjoyed the profit we made from it and considered purchasing another in the future. I came up with the idea to start our own trucking school offering one hundred percent job placement with CarDi.

Both men and women flocked to our school and became new drivers and/or dispatchers so that meant more loads delivered and more money made. I was making a salary in the high six figures and was loving it. California was good to me and good for me. It was absolutely great. Nothing and no one could hold me back. I was the man. I had dreams and big things were happening. Yeah, big things were happening.

CHAPTER 7

Diane

More than ever to prove...

The newspaper listed absolutely nothing that I was interested in. I was still a little down but part of me remained hopeful. Just then my own words to Marlene about calling my parents replayed in my head. Although I didn't win the contest I decided to call anyway just so I'd stop feeling guilty about leaving home the way I did, so I stepped out of my room and walked to the lounge down the hall to make the call. The phone rang about four times before someone picked up. To my surprise Sharon answered.

"Sharon? What are you doing at mom and dads?" I asked.

"Well, well, well," she said. "I see you have a lot more heart than I ever did. All I ever used to do was threaten to run away but you tell everybody in the house off then just up and leave the next morning," she said in an amused tone.

"Well, hi to you too, and it didn't exactly happen like that," I said.

"It doesn't matter how it happened just as long as you're okay," she said staying true to her cool big sister role. "Mom and dad are livid and can't believe you ran away the way you did. They say you should've told them so you could have left with their blessing," she said.

"Sharon, I hope you don't believe that. That doesn't even sound like something they'd say. Leave with their blessing. I've never heard anything remotely close to that coming out of either one of their mouths," I said snapping my head back and eyes wide with disbelief.

"Not for one second Sis. I know they would've fought you tooth and nail if you told them what you wanted to do," Sharon replied. "Even though you caused mom and dad stress I'm proud of you for venturing out on your own like that. Proud and jealous. Whoever heard of a big sister living vicariously through her baby sister?" she asked in a reflective tone.

Changing the subject, I asked where our parents were.

"Oh, mom is downstairs and dad left a few minutes ago to get a few things from the market."

"I thought you said they were stressed out," I asked.

"Well, they've been taking one day at a time while hoping and praying that you come back home or at least call. And their prayers were answered."

"What do you mean their prayers were answered?" I asked. "You neither I have ever seen or heard mom and dad praying about anything," I said in disbelief.

"Well, I've seen it myself and I've even prayed with them," she said.

"What on earth is going on?" I asked feeling like I was in the Twilight Zone. "I've only been gone about two weeks and already everyone's changing."

"Well I was changed way before you left."

"What do you mean when you say you were changed," I asked.

Sharon exhaled loudly preparing to speak. "I got saved."

"Oh that's nice," I said not wanting to delve any further into what Sharon had just revealed to me. After being preached to by Marlene I'd had enough of all the God and Jesus talk and I didn't want to cause friction between Sharon and I. "Even though I wanted to hurt mom and dad when I left because they wouldn't let me study music, I started feeling guilty so I called."

"Well praise God, we're just glad you're alright. I'm going to tell mom to pick up downstairs okay."

"Okay," I said feeling nervous to speak to my own mother.

"Well, hello there," my Mom said when she picked up the phone. My heart beat fiercely in my chest and my head thumped with my racing pulse.

"Hi," I said.

"Well, it's about time you called. Your daddy and I were worried about you. We were worried that something had happened. You ought to be asha..."

"Mom," Sharon cut in surprising Mom and I that she was still on the line. I was glad for her presence as mediator.

"I'm sorry," she said. "I'm just so happy that you're safe, but I'm also hurt that you didn't tell us to our faces that you were going to leave," she said.

My pulse racing, I took a deep breath to respond with a hot temper but Sharon cut in and said, "Guys, don't spend your time bickering. Mom, be glad that Diane is okay, that she's not in jail, been raped, or dead somewhere. Be glad that God kept her safe. I understand that you and dad are mad at her for leaving without telling you but you have to look at the situation from her perspective. You don't and have never supported her dream to sing. You said yourself in front of me plenty of times that you'll never help her pursue it. You guys got in an argument about it the day before she decided to leave. She tried talking to you guys one last time. She saw you wouldn't budge so she left. Now Diane, I understand the emotions that drove you to leave but leaving like that just wasn't the right thing to do. Now, I'm hanging up. I want you two to talk to each other without arguing."

"Click."

With that said I started speaking. "Mom, I never chose to sing. Singing chose me. I was born to do this. I know I was. There's nothing else I want to do. Sometimes it's both the greatest and the worst feeling at the same time because I long to do it but I've never been free to do it because you and daddy don't support me. I just want you and daddy to back me up and if you can't do that I'm still going to sing. Somehow, someway I'm going to do it."

"I see what you're saying," my Mom began, "but I want you to be able to have something that will enable you to pay your bills, keep up a mortgage and car payments. Your Dad and I aren't always going to be around and I want to leave this earth knowing you can take care of yourself. What type of income can living freely and living your dreams produce for you? I just can't see why you don't see that life is too short to not secure a promising career. You could spend too much time pursuing a singing career and not succeed. What'll happen if you get out there and you're singing and your career flops and you're not the "it girl" anymore and you run out of money, then what? I just think you're making a mistake allowing your heart to steer you and not your head."

"I see that you and I are never going to agree," I began, "and it's just going to be a waste of time continuing this conversation because we're going to continue to feel strongly about things and neither of us will bend. I think we should just agree to disagree because we've been down this road so many times before that I can walk it with my eyes closed."

"I'm telling you, you're going to regret this conversation one day," she said.

"Bye Mom," I said and hung up as she began to speak again. With that done, I could check it off my list of things I didn't want to do but did. I was deflated and energized at the same time. It was strange the way I was feeling. Although my mom had just reinforced the fact that she didn't support my career choice I was lighter in spirit and felt like I could focus better because I let go of the weight I carried, my parents.

"Hey girlie," a familiar voice said. I turned to see Carla decked out from head to toe.

"Girl, look at you!" I squealed jumping up to check out her clothes.

"You like?" she asked with a huge grin on her face.

"Oh come on now, you know I do. Look at my mouth dragging the ground. I'm salivating over here," I joked.

"Thanks, I just picked up this outfit at Viana's and every thing was so fly I decided to wear it out of the department store."

"Man, I wish I could dress like that," I sad admiring Carla's clothes.

"I still don't know why those judges didn't pick you, but you hang in there. Listen, I mentioned you to a friend of a friend I met at a party. I told him how cute you are, driven, and how powerful your voice is. He told me that he'd check some things out and let me know what he came up with."

"Oh my goodness, are you serious?!" I said grabbing Carla by the shoulders and shaking her.

"Yes, I am serious," she said straightening her jacket after I let go. "But relax, he hasn't gotten back to me yet."

"Girl, you don't know how thankful I am that you did this for me," I said gratefully.

"Hold on now, he hasn't said anything to me yet. I wasn't even going to tell you because it was right after I got casted for the movie and before your audition and I didn't know what your plans would be if you won," she said.

"Whatever, I'm just glad you did it because now I have some serious wheels in motion for me instead of the newspapers in my room. So, who's the friend and who's the friend of the friend?"

"Tsk, tsk, tsk," was the only sound I heard as Carla sucked her teeth three times chastising me. "Don't you know the person on the receiving end of a favor like this isn't supposed to ask questions?" she said in a playfully scolding voice.

"Sorry, I didn't know."

"Don't worry about it. I'll keep you posted and I'll let you know as soon as I hear something. I really do feel the gods are smiling down on you," she said matter of factly.

"The gods are smiling down on me?"

"Yeah, you know, things are looking up for you because the man upstairs has got your back." Grinning I stood up to follow Carla from the lounge to her room.

"I came to move the rest of my things from my room since I have a new place now," Carla said.

"Wow things are moving so quickly for you! I wish things were moving at the same pace for me," I said.

"Look, don't forget that I've been out here a little longer than you have. I've put in my time and now it's paying off."

"I guess you're glad that you held out and didn't give in to that guy that wanted to make you his property in exchange for a big break," I said.

"Mm-hmm," she said with her back turned as she folded clothes and placed them in bags.

"There's no way I'd ever sell my soul for a singing career because I'm too good for that," I said grabbing some clothes to help Carla.

"Yeah, uh, listen, Adam's waiting outside for me so I can't hang. I don't want whatever's left in the closet and on the dresser. I think there are a few things in the nightstand too. Help yourself to whatever you want and throw away what you don't. I'd rather throw them away than let anyone else here have them," she said.

"Will you ever stop by?" I asked feeling sad that my only friend was moving and leaving me behind.

"Honestly, I have no plans to come back here except to help you pack your things when you move out," she said grinning. "Here, she said pulling a piece of paper and a pen from her purse, "this is my new number. If another girl answers just tell her you're calling for me and she'll get me. If I'm not in leave a message with who ever it is and I'll call you back."

"Did you move to another boarding house or something?" I asked curiously.

"No, no. I have roommates that I share a condo with. The girls I live with either act, sing, model, or dance. It's cool living with them. You can visit sometime and I know you'll love it," she said descending the stairs with me trailing behind like a sad puppy.

"Okay, don't forget about the things in my room. Call me if you need me and I'll call you when I hear something." I guess how I was feeling showed up on my face because she reached out and hugged me. I hugged her back and looked out beyond her to Adam in his convertible. Carla turned and walked down the steps, as Adam waved and I waved back.

"See you soon!" he yelled.

"Okay, see you soon!" I yelled back as I waved even faster. Closing the door I looked around downstairs then headed upstairs to Carla's old room.

I started with the closet. There were a couple of tee-shirts and a jean jacket on one side and a yellow sundress on the other side. I took them off the hangers and threw them on the bed. I looked at the floor of the closet and saw several pairs of shoes. There were a few pairs of flats and two pairs of platforms, one brown and one maroon. I took both pairs of platforms and a black pair of flats. The things I wanted I threw on the bed and what I didn't want I threw into a pile on the floor.

I looked through everything, the dresser drawers, under the bed, and in the nightstand. I found a cute maroon purse in one of the dresser drawers that I decided to keep. Other than that she left behind a Bible, some socks, a couple pairs of already worn stockings, and some stationary. Having no use for those things I threw them to the pile on the floor. Holding everything tightly in my arms I took what I wanted to my room then went back with a paper bag and placed the other things inside.

I thought about putting the bag outside by the trash but people saw me walking to Carla's room with the bag and would probably go through it as soon as I turned my back. I rolled the top of the bag up and pushed the top down until the bag looked like a little footstool with no legs and slid it under my bed. I figured I'd throw it in the dumpster behind the diner the next day.

I was determined to keep my promise to Carla, no matter how small. I was grateful that she mentioned me to someone that could help me get on the fast track. I knew she'd be calling me soon to tell me the good news so the least I could do was throw her old clothes away like she asked.

CHAPTER 8

Diane

Chit-Chat

That night after dinner as I modeled my hand me downs from Carla I heard a knock at my door. Since no one in Marlene House ever visited my room except Carla and Marlene I knew who it was. Plus I'd come to know Marlene's knock pretty well in the week I'd been living there. Saying nothing, I got up and unlocked the door and walked back to my bed kicking off the second hand shoes I was wearing.

"Well, I guess you've come to hate me," Marlene said closing the door, walking toward me, and sitting on the bed. She turned to face me and mirrored my Indian-style position on the bed. A little surprised the shock showed on my face at Marlene's youthful behavior.

"What, you think the old girl couldn't get her legs up off the floor let alone fold them like this?" she said smiling warmly. I tried hard to ignore the smile but despite my not liking Marlene she was still strikingly beautiful. She looked as though she wanted to do some more sharing that I wasn't up to receiving. "I know you don't want to hear anything I have to say but that's my fault, at least partly my fault."

Thinking strongly about cutting her off, then opening my mouth to speak, Marlene held her hand up denoting she wanted a chance to talk uninterrupted.

"Thank you," she said smiling then shifted herself on the bed. "I feel that I've come at you the wrong way. I've come across as the overbearing mother type and I realize that in order for you to see me as a friend I have to be a friend, not a mother. I want to tell you about a woman I know very well. Me!" she said then touched her fingers to her chest. I'm originally from North Carolina and just like you I moved to California to pursue a dream. I wanted to sing. I could sing. I can sing.

84

Anyway, I was sixteen when I left North Carolina. I didn't know where I was going to live or how I was going to eat. Sixteen was old back then. Back then girls at that age had already been married with one or two children, but I wasn't thinking about getting married anytime soon because I was married to my music. I could sing and write and I was good, real good.

Back then it was so much harder for blacks, let alone a black woman trying to get a break. I think I would've had an easier time if I'd gone to New York though. At that time Billie Holiday, Lena Horne, Cab Calloway, and Duke Ellington were making a name for themselves. They were very popular. Ahh, the blues. Jazz. I loved it. Billie Holiday and I were both born in 1915, and Lena Horne was about two years younger, both beautiful women.

Anyhow, I made it to California and it was rough. I came during the summer which was the best thing about my decision to come here. I couldn't find a place to live so I lived on the streets. I was homeless for two weeks before an old Italian woman sat down next to me at a bus stop and started talking. I was surprised that she even acknowledged that I was sitting there. I was startled and was about to get up but she patted me on my thigh indicating that I should stay seated.

I didn't have any money left and was sitting there trying to figure out what I could do to get some so I could eat. I'd met a group of homeless kids just like me who came to California just like me hoping to become famous, hoping to get noticed- anything. One of them could sing and two of them could play the heck out of just about any instrument, and the other could dance real good.

Together they'd perform at different places as people walked by and gave them whatever they felt like giving. One of the guys noticed me one day because he thought I was pretty. We started talking and he invited me to meet his family as he called them. They ended up liking me and my singing enough to adopt me. That was nice of them. Whatever they made they split evenly amongst themselves and whatever was left over was put toward the next day's earnings.

It was nice being a part of their family but I wanted more. What I mean is pretty soon people were paying us more money because they wanted to hear me sing."

"How do you know people were paying more just to hear you sing?" I asked.

"Well, the more I sang the more there was to split because the crowds were getting larger. The next thing I knew, I wanted what I earned for myself so I could get off the streets. We ended up getting in an argument over it. One of the girls was kicked out because she sided with me. I felt bad and invited her to come with me, although I didn't know where I was going. She thought about it but declined. The group stuck together and protected each other. I found out about a month later that she'd been killed. She was doing her own thing in another part of the city and someone beat her to death for the little bit of money she'd earned. I never found out what happened to the rest of them, and we never knew each other's real names. They had nicknames for each other since they'd been together for a while. When I came along they called me Black Diamond."

"That was a pretty name," I said thinking that it fit Marlene even to this day.

"Yeah, it was. Sitting on that bench I tried to make myself forget how hungry I was and how fowl I smelled. My clothes were becoming dirty again and I had no money for the laundry mat. Sometimes it was either stink and be dirty or have a full stomach. The woman turned to me and asked me how I was doing and I told her fine. She asked where I was going and I said I didn't know. She must've smelled me or something because the next thing she said was that she had a hot shower and tub. When I looked up she added that she made a big pot of stew and had a clean bed with crisp, cool sheets that I was welcome to if I wanted them.

"I know you don't have a place to go," she said. "Come home with me. The street and alleyways are no place for a young girl. Come." She could've been an axe murderer for all I knew but what she had to offer was more than what I had so I went.

On the way she asked me about myself and I told her everything. In exchange for a place to stay all I had to do was clean, run errands, and keep her company. She taught me how to play all sorts of card games. You notice I didn't say cook because that old woman could throw down in the kitchen! I loved her.

Several months after moving in I earned my diploma after taking night classes at a nearby school. Before I knew it two years passed without me singing a note outside of the house. When I turned eighteen it was time for me to get started on my singing career. I continued to live with Mom, that's what I called her, as I tried to get my name out there.

It was hard but after a few years I got my foot in the door. It was a little door but it was something. My first gig was singing backup for a group called Smooth. It was a good experience and I got exposure. People were seeing me and there were times I had little solo parts. Mostly I sang at night clubs with them for about a year. Not long after that the group leader and one of the back up singers ran off and got married leaving me, the other back up singer, and the musicians. We felt lost until we discovered a girl named Georgette at a club we frequented when we weren't performing.

At first we thought about replacing the lead position with another guy but by a unanimous decision our group chose me as the new lead and Georgette would take my place as back up. Since I had more creative freedom singing lead I felt it was time to present some of the songs I'd written to see what kind of response I'd get from my band. They liked a lot of them. Pretty soon we were singing song after song that I wrote. The crowds loved us when we performed.

I was so elated that things began to go to my head. After awhile and I wasn't a very nice person to be with. My group let me know too but I just brushed them off and chalked all that talk and whining up to them being a bunch of jealous folk who only wished they were as talented as me. At night I'd lay in bed evaluating each member of my band to determine if anyone was really a threat to me, was really competition, and every night I fell asleep with a grin of satisfaction knowing my group couldn't make it without me even if they tried.

Then one day I showed up to practice and everyone was offstage sitting around like something had happened. "What's going on?" I asked curious to know why a couple of them wouldn't look me in the eye.

The drummer spoke up, "We took a vote to kick you out of the group," he said not beating around the bush. "Black Diamond is a group. It is not a bunch of kids of an overbearing stepmother," he said. "You talk to us like we have no talent of our own, like you can be Black Diamond all by yourself. We demand respect and won't tolerate you yelling at us like some dogs. This isn't the first time we've mentioned this to you so you're out," he said staring daggers at me.

"Yall are kidding right? That's what's going on. Yall are kidding. Ha! Ha! Ha!" I laughed. "You really had me going for a minute there. This is so funny!" Understanding they were for real after getting a good look at them I realized I was in trouble. "Okay, alright, I'm sorry, and I apologize. It won't happen again," I said in a weak attempt to change their minds once again. But this time they meant it. Trembling inside but stoic outside I said, "Okay, I'm leaving but I'm taking my name and my music. Whatever I gave to this group is leaving with me!" Then the thought came to me about recruiting for my new band and I had the audacity to ask if anyone wanted to come with me. One of the girls came and the piano player came leaving the drummer, Georgette, and the guitarist. Satisfied that I'd stripped the band of as much as I could I walked and reformed Black Diamond.

So there we were me, my back up singer, and a pianist. I was into jazz and the blues but between the two the blues had my heart. My daddy left my mama, me, and my brothers and sisters, then my mama left us with our grandparents to find a man and a good job but she forgot all about us. I guess life was good without having all those extra mouths to feed.

Eventually Black Diamond got it together. We hired a bass player and we did what we did best... perform. Now, me and my back up singer Pauline became very close because we spent so much time together. She was my home girl. She was a few years older than me and had been singing much longer than me too. She started off in church like a lot of singers do, and she was a lot of fun. I know you've never heard anything about me or my group but we were famous in the thirties and forties. We traveled around the world too. We were making money and enjoying life.

Well, we were enjoying life as much as we could living on the road yet wanting to have lasting relationships that were always out of our grasp. Then one day Pauline introduced me to the party scene. I mean we already went to clubs or wherever there was a party worth going to but this party was different. One night Pauline and I got decked out in our baddest clothes and went to a private club called Christine's. We met up with some people she knew that took us to a back room where people were doing all kinds of drugs and other things. I'd never done anything like that before and was nervous and curious at the same time.

The room was dimly lit and there was music playing so loud that it seemed like it was going through me. We continued walking across the room and sat down on a couch next to a few people. There were some chairs around a coffee table along with the couch we sat on. I felt out of place but Pauline looked like this place was her home away from home. Everyone else was leaned back against the back of whatever they were sitting on and those that weren't sitting on chairs were leaned against the wall or lying spread out on the floor. I don't know how we didn't step on any of them. In contrast to everyone's relaxed state I was sitting straight up holding onto my purse and at the edge of the couch cushion.

Everyone around the coffee table was inhaling something from some device and it was passed to me four or five times before I let go and decided to try it. I tried it and immediately it gently laid me back against the back of the couch and I never missed my turn again whether we were there, at my place, at Pauline's, or me by myself. I was hooked. I was so bad that I think I was on cloud nine twenty-four seven."

"You? You were getting high?" I asked taking in every word Marlene said.

"Yes I was. Now listen to my story. One day I realized I was an addict. It was not because I examined myself but because Pauline was my mirror. I used to sit and look at Pauline as she and I got high sharing the same needles and I used to think how ugly and worn out she'd become. She was always tired and slack in the mouth and her singing wasn't great anymore. I was thinking of letting her go. Huhhh, oh how I wish I could go back and change some things around."

Chapter 9

Marlene's Story
Okay God, I hear you!

One day Pauline and I sat facing each other getting high and the tracks on her arms had them so bruised and battered. Her legs too had become pin cushions and I was disgusted by the sight and smell of her. I remember being upset with her.

"Get up, why don't you get up and wash! Look at you, you're not beautiful anymore! You're no good that's what you are! You can't even open your mouth wide enough to back me up properly! You stink! Everyone knows you're on that stuff but I'm not keeping it a secret!" I said woozily standing and pulling my arm back through the neck of my shirt. "You're disgusting!" I screamed. Pauline looked at me and laughed as if I hadn't just shared what I said.

"You know, you always thought you were better than everybody else," she said as her head dangled from her noodle neck. "All you gotta do is look at me to see you," she said wiping her nose with the back of her ashy hand and curling up like a baby on the bed. Furious, I told her to get out of my house and get out of my life. I told her she was no longer a part of Black Diamond and she laughed.

"Black Diamond, you think people care about Black Diamond anymore? Nobody cares about us anymore and I don't care that they don't. All I care about is this," she said wearily fingering a needle and piece of rubber. "This here is my mother that had so many kids that her love ran out for me to cover them. *This* is always here for me like my daddy wasn't. *This* is the justice I deserve for being a mattress for all the filthy drunks my mother tried to turn into daddies for us. *This* here is my church because church folk don't want me sitting on their pews. They don't come to me so I go to them but they don't want me cause my skirt is too tight and

90

the mask I put on everyday to hide the pain makes them want me or hate me for being wanted. *This* is my god because it answers all my prayers by taking the pain away... all the pain away. Wherever I get down with this is my church. *This* is all I need in life."

"Get outta here talking like that!" I yelled.

"I'll leave but I aint saying goodbye because I know I'll be seeing you again when you run out. Right now you feel like Superman because you just scored but we'll be friends again," she said grabbing her purse and shoes, heading toward my front door.

"Bye junkie!" she yelled out before slamming my door.

"Ahhhhh! I screamed until my head hurt and my lungs ran out of air. I knew Pauline was right. Pauline was right many times after that. She was right about other things too. No one came to see Black Diamond anymore. Sold out shows were no more and then the articles started popping up. Truthfully I'm surprised they didn't surface sooner. My musicians left the group dissolving my dream. I lost everything! I lost my house, my car, my status, my money, my hopes and dreams. I had nothing. I had no one but Mrs. Petitti.

See, my life in North Carolina was similar to Pauline's and that's why we got along so well. My mother had six kids one after the other and the next thing I knew I was mother to my brothers and sisters as the oldest. One night my daddy went out for a drink and never came back. Some say he couldn't take not being able to support all of us so he left to make a better life for himself. I heard years later that he got remarried and became a stepfather to his wife's children. The type of father he should've been to us.

I did all I could for my family by checking on them and sending money every week. I put all my brothers and sisters through college and I'm proud of that. That's about all I can look back at and be proud of.

Just before I lost it all Pauline and I were celebrating the new year together out on the town. We were feeling good because we'd both decided to drop that stuff and get ourselves together. We were gonna do it together. After that we planned to form another band and hit the road again. Yet despite all the planning neither of us said anything about it but I knew we both planned to get high just one more time before changing our lives around.

We stepped outside to the alley to shoot up. She first, then I slid down the wall with my back pressed against it and settled in next to Pauline like so many times before. In my stupor I murmured silly things to my friend about how wild that night was gonna be and I hate remembering what happened next.

"Pauline! Pauline! Girl, you better get yourself together and come on. We got some partying to do and some plans to make!" I said waving my hands in the air and dancing from the waist up. "Okay, so the plan is we're checking into the place tomorrow morning then… Pauline? Oh my God! Pauline no!" I yelled turning toward her. "Pauline no! Oh Lord Jesus no! No! No! Noooo!"

I shook her over and over and over but she never woke up. All the shaking in the world wouldn't return her spirit to her body. Pauline's body fell over to its right side, her head landing sideways on a trash bag as if she were using it for a pillow. I'd felt so invincible before then but while standing over Pauline's lifeless body in the dark of the alley, life and death became real to me and I wished Pauline didn't have to be the one to teach me that lesson.

I wished it was another pastor, minister, missionary, church member, anybody witnessing to me like so many times before but I just flipped them off and walked away in the middle of their talking, and some in the middle of their prayers for me. Every now and then I'd listen to what they said or what they were praying to God for on my behalf. They prayed that God would touch my heart so I'd be drawn to Him, that He would open my eyes and ears so I would hear and understand His word. They prayed that I would hear the voice of His Holy Spirit and obey. But at that time I didn't want to hear anything God had to say.

After Pauline overdosed, I found myself for the first time in my life yelling out to God, "I'm listening!" I knew Pauline was still a reflection of me but her end didn't have to be mine. Taking one last look at Pauline I turned and ran to my car that was on its last leg and didn't start. I took my personal things from it and said goodbye. I walked to the bus stop and wondered where I'd go. Surely I couldn't go to Mrs. Petitti looking like a dirty mop, but if she loved me like she said she'd take me in regardless and take care of me like before.

I searched my purse for bus fare dropped it in the box, then walked slowly to my seat and sat down. After a moment, I realized that my lap was bouncing my shaky hands. I stilled my legs then sat on my hands to ease their trembling. Sadly, I sat there afraid for my own life wondering why Pauline collapsed like that and why I had to see it and have it forever burned in my mind.

I wondered if I was going to be the next example for someone else and tried to calm myself down, but after attempting to calm down I jumped at the thought of my heart stopping. I was a mess and suddenly afraid that I would be the next one to die. I had to go to Mrs. Petitti because my family looked up to me. It would kill them to see me messed up and it would kill my pride to allow them to see me.

CHAPTER 10

Marlene's Story
Getting to know Him

I'd visited Mrs. Petitti many times since moving out but I was afraid to let her see me looking so bad because her little Leenie knew better. Stepping off the bus and walking to Mrs. Petitti's street I rehearsed what I was going to say, however, nothing I rehearsed was good enough by the time I reached the door. To my surprise the knob didn't turn and I stumbled backward onto the first step to get a good look at the house and address to make sure I was at the right one. It was the right one so I knocked on the door. I knocked again and still no answer.

It started to drizzle and I needed to go indoors so I walked around to the side of the house and tried my key to the cellar. It worked. There was a cot in the back corner and a blanket and pillow were neatly situated on it. I reached out and picked up a long nightgown, socks, and a robe. I undressed and changed. When I walked to the door that lead to the rest of the house I smiled thinking of my second mother's love for me but when I reached the door to turn the knob I was struck in the face with the hard realization once again, that my secret wasn't a secret and that junkies can be loved but not trusted. The knob didn't turn.

Mrs. Petitti came down in the morning and stood over me wearing a loving look on her face in place of the disgust I feared I'd see. When I stood up to hug her that was the beginning of my recovery, but it took several months for me to beat my addiction for good. There were times I thought I was gong to die but I beat the addiction and was set free. Now that I was reduced to nothing I had to assess my life and start over.

Mrs. Petitti, who I began calling mom told me I had to get up and get a job to support myself. At twenty-four, the only jobs I'd ever had were babysitting my brothers and sisters and singing. Singing. Once it was something that brought excitement and that funny feeling in your stomach when you're anxious to get started with something that you've been looking forward to doing. Now singing left a sour taste in my mouth.

Thinking of singing returned my mind to Black Diamond, which reminded me of Pauline, and both memories made plain that I'd made some terrible mistakes and wasn't immortal because I could fall prey to them at any moment. I thought about packing up and leaving L.A. to start over someplace else where there were no memories of where my life rose and fell. I dreaded the flashbacks every time I passed a building, bar, store, or restaurant that I used to frequent with the band or Pauline. Not only that, but my appearance reminded me of my addiction everyday.

Mom said it was all in how I interpreted what was around me. Instead of feeling sorry and defeated I could gain strength from good memories but learn from the bad ones. So that's what I did. I stayed. I had some trouble finding a job on my own but mom asked around until her friend's daughter Betty agreed to hire me to clean her home. I did not want to be a maid or a housekeeper because I felt it was beneath me. I thought I was being ridiculed because of my past success and my race.

Mom helped me to see that at that time in my life I needed that. I needed to be humbled after all I went through. I threw away my ability to work for myself and not be told what to do. At first I didn't know how to take Betty because she didn't say much to me other than good morning, good afternoon, and good bye. Beside those things she'd go over my daily list of things to do before going to another part of the house or leaving for the store or wherever else she went during the day.

After working for Betty for about two months she stood in the doorway of the bathroom I was cleaning and watched me clean the mirror over the sink. No one likes being watched while they work but because Betty never did it for the exception of the first week I started, I didn't mind. She finally spoke and said she might have another job for me if I wanted it.

"Everyday I go to my church to help out here and there and I just found out that one of the ladies quit because of health reasons. If you'd like you can take her place to make some extra money. Are you interested?" Standing there it didn't seem that I had much time to make up mind, so I said yes. "Oh good. I've already mentioned you to the other ladies there and they're looking forward to meeting you. You can start tomorrow afternoon," she said smiling and taking one last look at me before turning and walking off.

The next day was like any other day except around eleven that morning

Betty called me to get my things to go to her church. I followed her out the door and to her car where she indicated for me to sit up front with her. The church was about fifteen minutes away and was one of those big stone buildings with cathedral ceilings, stone steps, stained glass windows, and wooden floors. Inside the church was beautiful. I took it all in because I'd only been inside a church a few times in my life, Pauline's funeral being the last.

I assumed Betty was Catholic for some reason although you can't tell what religion someone is by looking at them unless they're wearing clothing or articles that are associated with their form of worship. I continued walking slowly through the church along the wall on the right side and I observed everything. I saw nothing indicating that I was in a Catholic church, not that it would matter, but I was curious. I saw no Mary holding a broken, battered, bruised, and bloody Jesus and whatever else I thought I'd see.

We then entered a room and approached a door that was closed and I heard voices on the other side. As we got closer I realized the people on the other side were praying. We stood there a moment then the woman that was praying when we walked up finished and a man picked up where she left off. He was praying for safety. Two other people prayed then everyone's voice was heard as they all prayed together. Then I heard the most unusual noises or talking. I was dumbfounded because they all started speaking in another language. I'd traveled to many different cities in many countries and heard many different languages, but I'd never heard the language these people were speaking and after listening very carefully I could tell that they were each saying something different.

I was totally confused and filled with questions after hearing that. A few moments later The door opened and everyone in the room filed out and went in different directions in the church. At that moment Betty introduced me to a woman named Millicent and left to do whatever her task at the church was. Millicent was nice and liked to talk so I didn't feel awkward later on asking her about what I heard during their prayer time.

"Oh you mean earlier?" she asked in a bubbly voice.

"Yes, when you all were in the room taking turns praying," I said feeling anxious about her response.

"Oh, we were speaking in tongues, I mean praying in our Heavenly prayer language."

Her response both interested me and startled me at the same time. I had never heard of speaking in tongues or a Heavenly prayer language and wondered if those people were crazy or apart of some cult or something else weird.

"How did you learn how to speak it?" I asked.

"You don't learn how to speak in your Heavenly prayer language. Your own language is given to you as a gift from God. You should speak it everyday to develop it, but like I said it's not something you learn. All you have to do is receive it like someone is standing in front of you with their arms extended toward you holding a present. Then all you have to do is reach out and take it," she explained. "That's how I was able to begin speaking in tongues. The church I used to go to before this one didn't believe in speaking in tongues. Honestly, I'm not exactly sure what they believed because they were all over the place with God's word. God's word is His word and is not to be interpreted to satisfy our own desires. That church either believed that speaking in tongues isn't for everyone or it was only for the people in the Bible days in the New Testament."

Millicent was talking a mile a minute and I was completely lost. I was drowning in her sea of words and my mind was grasping for something, anything to hold onto so I could understand her and follow what she was saying.

"What's wrong with just praying a regular prayer? Why do you pray in a Heavenly prayer language when you can pray in English?

"Good questions. I'm glad you asked. See, when we pray out loud in English or whatever your native language is, I can hear what you're saying as well as everyone else. Not only that, but the devil can hear you too. When he hears what we pray about he tries to hinder our prayers. Plus, when we pray in English we're praying with our mind and based on our desires. But when we're filled with the Holy Spirit, the Holy Spirit examines us and our life and causes us to pray for things we didn't even know we needed to pray for. For example, if there's something going on in your body that you didn't know about, the Holy Spirit will speak to your spirit and you will pray for yourself not knowing anything about the issue. Oftentimes the Holy Spirit has us praying for other people as well. Oh, and even more exciting is if you're praying in your regular language and you feel the urge to begin praying in your "Heavenly Language" that's an indicator that you've touched on a subject that the Holy Spirit wants you to pray in the spirit about. To top it all off, the devil doesn't understand what you're saying when you pray in the spirit, so he can't eavesdrop and try to hinder your prayers. It's all so very wonderful!" she explained excitedly.

"Millicent, can you tell me more about how you understand all this and can I hear you pray?"

"Oh sure," she said excitedly. Whatever it was it lit Millicent up, but then again she could've just been a naturally bubbly and excitable person.

"First of all you need to make up in your mind that you want to change."

"Want to change what?" I asked innocently.

"That you want to change your life around and not live a life of sin," she said."

Not wanting to seem completely dense about the subject I said, "I don't know much but I do know that everyone sins, no one can help it."

"True but you have to be at a point in your life where you decide that you want to be forgiven of your sins and live for Jesus. You have to first realize that you're a sinner, and once you realize that there's a special prayer you pray asking Jesus to come into your heart and forgive you of your sins. After doing that you you're forgiven for all the sins you've ever committed then you can move on to receiving the Holy Ghost," she said happily as if she'd already mentioned it.

"The Holy Ghost? What on earth is that?" I asked totally puzzled.

"It's the same thing as saying the Holy Spirit just another way of saying it."

"Oh," I said confused just as I thought I was beginning to understand everything.

When we were just about finished with our work, looking at me and touching my arm Millicent said, "Don't worry Marlene, before long it'll all make sense, you'll see. You're going to be saved and filled with the Holy Spirit because I'm going to help you." With that she smiled and squeezed my hand.

Just then Betty came walking up and smiled. It seemed like everyone was smiling. I even noticed as people were walking around they seemed to have a peacefulness about them. I saw some black men and women working and smiling and whistling and they all had menial jobs just like me. They probably never had nor would they ever lay eyes on the money I used to make. Why were they so happy when they had no reason to be?

Although I still had a few hours until my work day was over Betty drove me home saying I could have a short day. "Thanks," I said getting out of her car and shutting the door. Upstairs in my room I thought about the things I heard that day and what Millicent said. I wanted to talk to Mom about it but she never, ever said anything about God, church, praying, or anything. I wanted to be able to discuss these things with someone else beside Millicent so I could compare what she said to what someone else had to say about Jesus and the Holy Spirit.

I was only scheduled to work at the church three times a week, every other day so I wouldn't be seeing Millicent for another two days. My mind went to my conversation with her often and it bothered me. That night lying in bed I couldn't sleep and I didn't understand why I kept dwelling on the things Millicent told me. Questions like why do I need to be saved? What am I being saved from? And how do I get saved kept replaying in my mind over and over. I felt like I was going to go crazy until I got the crazy idea to talk to God or whoever was there.

"I don't know who I'm talking to. God, Jesus, the Holy Spirit, or the Holy Ghost, or whoever. I don't know what to believe. I didn't grow up around church folk and now I'm hearing stuff about being saved and changing my life and sins and I'm confused and concerned. Confused because there seems to be so much information to understand and it sounds like there are a lot of steps involved. Are you real? Do you really exist? And I'm concerned because there are many things out there to believe. Why should I believe anything about you? If you are real show me that you're real. You're real to Millicent and you must be real to the other people at the church. There's something there. I want to be happy for no reason too. Umm, that's all I have to say. Uh, goodnight."

The next day, I worked with Millicent we talked a little more and I kept asking questions. I learned that God's word says that He loves us so much He gave His very best to us, His son Jesus Christ, to die in our place for our sins because the punishment for sinning is death. Just like I said that everyone sins, everyone needs to be forgiven of their sins and only the blood of Jesus can do it. God says that all we have to do is believe in Jesus His son. We just have to believe that Jesus allowed our sins to be placed on Him along with all of our shame and died in our place because he took our punishment for us. This is powerful because Jesus was the very last sacrifice needed to take sin away. Once Jesus died there was no reason to sacrifice lambs and other animals because Jesus' blood forever flows upon the altar in Heaven.

Then believing that He died in our place we must believe that He was resurrected, defeated death and is forever alive as we will be if we believe in Him. After I prayed and told God that I believe in Jesus and asked Him to forgive me of my sins I cried. I cried because everything I'd ever done was forgiven and everything I'll ever do has been covered as well. That doesn't mean that I can live my life whatever way I want to and just keep asking for forgiveness, but it means that if I mess up, and I will because I'm human, that all I have to do is tell God I'm sorry, learn from my mistake, and keep moving forward.

After I repeated the prayer of forgiveness with Millicent she prayed with me to receive the Holy Spirit. She told me to visualize Jesus giving me a present and inside was the Holy Spirit. She said I had to want it and I had to understand that Jesus wanted to give it to me. I wanted it so bad because Millicent told me how wonderful it is to speak in her Heavenly prayer language and how the Holy Spirit helps you to pray and gets involved in ever area of your life.

My eyes were closed and in my mind I pictured Jesus handing me a beautifully wrapped present and as Millicent was praying she had her hand on my head and told me to raise both my hands. I was nervous and excited at the same time. My heart was still pounding from becoming saved just a few moments before that. When Millicent finished praying she told me to start praying. I hesitated so she quickly told me to keep repeating "Thank you Jesus, thank you Jesus."

She said the Holy Spirit would come and do the rest and that I'd know because my mouth and tongue would begin moving on their own. Then it was as if the atmosphere changed because I felt my top lip twitch and tingle then my tongue began to move on it's own in a fluttering motion and "thank you Jesus" became gibberish. What I was saying didn't make sense to me but what I was saying flowed from deep inside me out of my mouth and tears fell freely from my eyes as God became more real to me. His Holy Spirit became real to me that day and Millicent and I prayed in our Heavenly language for a few minutes more.

It was new and it was beautiful and Millicent's tongue rolling sounds were so different from the sounds I was making and she sounded so powerful and confident as I stammered and stuttered but I didn't care because I got it! I got it! Afterward I wiped the tears from my eyes and Millicent hugged me. I felt so, so clean and so right inside and so light. I felt like I could float. I've been saved ever since.

CHAPTER 11

Diane

I hear what you're saying but...

Sitting quietly for a moment Marlene looked down at her hands and examined them as if they were new, looking at the dark backs then at the bright palms. Engrossed with her hands myself, I was startled when I saw a tear splash onto the back of one of them. I'd been lost in her story and didn't realize she was becoming human to me while sitting across from me on my bed. Touched by her emotion and ashamed at how I'd been disrespecting her, I touched her hand. She sniffed and lifted the lower right corner of her apron to dry her nose. After she got herself together she spoke again.

"I was twenty-four then and I'm sixty now, so that was thirty-six years ago."

"Wow," I said not knowing what else to say. "You had an interesting life."

"A lot more happened too but the things I talked to you about are the things that pertain mostly to you. Don't let your dream to sing and bad decisions ruin your life. Don't allow anyone to steer you in the wrong direction. Now, Pauline and Carla may not be exactly alike because I think Carla's worse, so you take heed to what I went through. I'm telling you this hoping you'll think about the things I did so you don't have to experience the pain I experienced, or worse. I want to be the Millicent in your life. I used to wish that Pauline and I met Millicent before we started making all of our bad decisions. I want to be the Millicent in your life now before you get off track," Marlene said.

I guess the look on my face revealed my conflicted thoughts. I wanted to sing R&B but from what Marlene was telling me I couldn't do that. It would be a sin. I would not be living my life for Christ, but singing was more important to me than walking around saved and praying in tongues. I'd heard a little about that at Celeste's church, but I didn't need all that in my life at the moment because I was young and not gullible and weak like Marlene was.

"Thanks Marlene but I'm not ready for all that yet," I said.

"I know; you're young and you have your whole life ahead of you. I'm not going to pressure you but if you want to talk about anything, and I mean anything you can talk to me," she said looking at me seriously. Too seriously. "One more thing, make sure that whoever you get advice from has your best interest at heart. I'm telling you this because I care about you. You remind me of myself at your age. You can come to me," she said unfolding her long black legs and resting her feet on the floor.

She stretched and arched her back backward rubbing her lower back while standing. "Try not to forget what I said," and she left me alone with my thoughts. Really there was nothing to think about on my end. I was just recapping all the things Marlene experienced when she was younger. I was giving some serious thought to quitting my job at the diner since I knew there was no way whoever it was Carla had spoken to wouldn't be interested in someone as talented as me. I think the contest must've been fixed or something, but I am without a doubt prepared to do anything to be famous and perform on stages before millions of people all over the world. To me, that was the greatest high. Marlene was crazy to throw all that away.

I'm not going back to that diner. That's no place for a future star. I'm going to use some of the money I won today to live off of for a while until Carla's connection calls her back.

Feeling good about my decision to quit the diner I hopped off my bed and headed for my car. I made up in my mind that I should look the part before I even got the call from Carla, so I picked up a few new outfits, I purchased some shoes, matching purses, some maxis, new makeup, and whatever else I felt a future star should have.

"I'm waiting for your call Carla. Please call," I said out loud to myself.

CHAPTER 12

Diane

I'm on my way...

Before I knew it a week passed by but there was no word from Carla. Then two more weeks passed by, then a whole month. After that fourth week I started to get nervous and anxious, then a few days later, I got a call.

"Diane!" someone from the lounge down the hall from my room yelled, "it's for you!" I ran down the hall almost snatching the receiver from the guy's hand. "Hello, hello!" I said. "Oh girl I was starting to get worried. I thought you'd never call. A few days more and I was going to call you!"

"Well girlie, I have the news you've been waiting so patiently for," she said dangling the information in front of me. "Okay, the guy who's interested in helping you is Carlton Levy. He says he wants to meet you very soon, like in a couple days, well, Thursday actually."

"Okay, where do I meet him?" I asked.

"A car will be sent to pick you up," she said as if I was used to being chauffeured around.

"What time?" I asked.

"Three o'clock." And make sure you pack an overnight bag because you're staying with me!" she said excitedly.

"Oh my goodness! I can't believe this is happening! I can't believe it! I owe everything to you Carla, do you know how much this means to me?" I asked.

"Okay, okay, don't go getting all serious on me now. Just make sure you wear something nice for your meeting with Carl. I know he'll fall in love with you when he sees you. Just be yourself and know he's just as excited to see you as you are to meet him," she said as words of wisdom.

"Alright I'll be ready and waiting."

"Make sure you're ready to go by three o'clock. The car will be there then. I'll talk to you on Thursday unless something comes up."

"I hope nothing comes up," I said. We ended the call then I skipped back to my room wondering which of my new outfits I was going to wear, how my hair was going to be styled and anything else I could manage to worry over. When I got to my room I closed the door and pressed my back against it, then found myself thanking God and asking that everything work out for my good.

Those really weren't my words but part of a prayer I'd heard Celeste's mom pray a few times. That's how I felt so I said those words. I'd never really prayed before beyond the normal things that people say like "oh my God," or "thank God," or "God bless you". For a second I felt a little guilty, at least that's the first thing that came to mind when I uttered that payer.

I went through my closet plowing through clothes. I had no idea what I should wear to meet the man that was going to change my life forever.

The next day Carla happened to call back and asked if I decided on an outfit and I told her no. She said she thought of me and picked something up as a gift since she knew my size. Not only that but she was picking me up later to get my hair and nails done. I was floored at how generous Carla was and truly thankful for a friend like her. A little later in the day Carla came by and got me. She told me I might as well stay over at her place after getting dolled up. It made more sense since Mr. Levy was closer to her place than Marlene House.

I opened the door to her car and threw my overnight bag in the backseat. Grinning from ear to ear, I reached over and hugged Carla as she put the car in gear and drove off. During the ride I rattled on and on about how excited I was, then Carla had to tell me to calm down. We arrived at the salon and Carla helped me pick....no Carla suggested a hairstyle to get because she knew Carl's taste. She also suggested a fiery red polish for my fingers and toes. Neither were my taste but I trusted Carla's judgment and believed she knew what she was doing. The bottom line was I wanted to impress Mr. Carl Levy at all costs.

Later that evening, Carla and I ate out then headed back to her condo. Upon entering the foyer I smelled different scents I'd never smelled before. Seeing me scrunch up my nose then cover it Carla cleared her throat but she never addressed the obvious scents. Walking through the house I took everything in like the bright colors on the walls, the art, the carpet and wood flooring, the furniture and the people. There was music playing loudly in a room at the end of a hall and I heard glasses clinking and laughter here and there.

"And here we are," Carla said after we climbed the stairs and reached a bedroom door. She opened it and my mouth flew open. She had a huge bed with big, soft pillows on it. Each wall was painted a different color as if a clown decorated the room, but it was all so amazing to me. Seeing my surprise and awe she said, "When I was a little girl I always wanted a room exactly like this. I wanted lots of pillows, a huge, huge bed, and lots and lots of color. As soon as I moved in Adam said I could have the room I wanted."

"Wow, you're so lucky to have a boyfriend like Adam. Does he have any brothers or cousins or something?" I asked half joking and half meaning it.

Laughing and patting a corner chair she said, "You can sit your things here. I'm still waiting for an extra bed to come so you can be comfortable during your stay."

"Oh, I don't want to be any trouble. I can sleep right here on the floor. If you give me a few blankets and a pillow I can make a pallet and be just as comfortable."

"Girl, where did you say you're from again? I haven't heard anyone but my parents and grandparents talk about a pallet on the floor and that's because they grew up dirt poor in the south!" she said laughing. I had no response except to laugh and tell her to shut up.

After I'd been there an hour Carla got down to business telling me what Mr. Levy was like and what he liked and didn't like. I felt like I was going to be sold at an auction or something the way she made such a big fuss over the whole thing. I was excited but Carla was a little over the top. Next she pulled out the outfit she picked up for me. It was a beautiful red sequenced dress that was so short I was afraid to breathe for fear that all my stuff could be seen. The dip at the neck was so low that if I pulled my chin close enough to my chest I could make out my belly button.

"This is what you picked out?" I asked with a hint of disappointment in my voice and I hoped nothing on my face.

"Yeah, don't you like it? She asked.

"Well, it's a little too much for me, or better yet, not enough. I mean I've never worn anything like this before. The dress is ridiculously short and this dip is way too low and..." I said backing up toward a full length mirror next to her closet, "I can just about make out a butt cheek and the beginning of my butt crack. I can't wear this," I said exasperated and feeling let down.

"Hold on. You look beautiful in this dress. I happen to know that Carl has a weakness for beauty and I want you to show yours off. I happen to know that you're not the only girl he met with this week. I had my eyes and ears open to know what he liked and disliked about each girl. By knowing those things I picked out your hairstyle, nail color, and outfit. Don't be worried. This may not be you, but you'll only have to wear it for a short time. After that you can go back to being you," she said reassuringly. Touching me on my shoulder she convinced me to smile and I did. "Are we still cool?" she asked.

"Yeah, we're still cool," I said sliding a strap back onto my shoulder. "Now where were we?" I asked as I turned around to face the full length mirror. We spent another hour or so on my dress and heels and hair then finally we changed into more comfortable clothes.

"There's one more thing I forgot to mention," she said. My stomach churned a little after hearing her speak. "Carl may offer you a drink".

"And?" I asked knowing Carla knew that I didn't drink.

"I think you should accept it and drink it. Just take a few sips. I know for a fact that he's going to offer you something and if you turn it down he's going to be offended. Just take the glass, be relaxed, and go with the flow," she said coaching me.

"Carla the more you tell me about this meeting the more worried I get. Why does this man want so much from me? I mean, why can't I just show up in something less provocative and why am I changing everything about me? You haven't even said anything about him wanting to hear me sing," I said standing up to pace the floor.

"Listen, you were the one that was excited when I told you I'd put in a good word for you and now you're acting all childish over a stupid dress and a drink. Is it too much to ask? Because if it is then maybe the music industry isn't the place for you to be. And on top of that Carl stayed out here a little longer just to meet you," she said with annoyance in her voice. "Think about me for a minute, I'm the new girl around here and I'm asking for favors already . If you don't care about anything else at least care about whether or not you make me look bad around here. I was accepted for the part but we haven't begun filming yet. There's nothing stopping them from kicking me out and bringing the next girl in if they think I'm going to be as difficult to deal with as you. You yourself know how many people want their big break just from being in that singing contest. Don't mess this up," she said looking at me.

Feeling bad about how I behaved I apologized for acting so childishly and blamed it on being nervous. That was true. But only in part. I didn't like feeling as though I was going to be examined. Nonetheless, I was going to do it and whatever else I had to do to live my dream. The next day went by unbelievably fast and before I knew it I was dressing for my meeting with Mr. Levy.

With a final brush of my hair I added some gloss and blotted my lips for the perfect look, and then Carla stood in front of me with a bottle of what looked to be expensive perfume. She sprayed a huge mist of it above me and I knew from experience to hold my arms out and spin around slowly allowing the beautifully scented perfume to land on me like millions of tiny raindrops.

"You'll be great," she said as we walked to the front door.

"Good luck," I heard two female voices say from the den as we stepped outside to walk to a waiting limo. Carla was riding with me and would wait for me to finish meeting with Mr. Levy. I was so grateful for all of Carla's support yet I couldn't wait until the meeting was over. On the way, Carla explained that Mr. Levy had many homes all over the world and that we'd be meeting at one of his California homes. Somehow knowing that made me feel a little more at ease and not so much like I was going to an interview.

The limo finally pulled in front of the most beautiful home I'd ever seen. It was white and had many windows. It was a magnificent sight, and the mountains in the distance added to the painting-like vision I beheld. My heart racing I put my hand on the door handle but was startled when it opened suddenly from outside. I'd forgotten that that's the sort of thing a chauffeur does. I looked over at Carla and she patted my hand that was still on the seat between the two of us. My hands were sweating and I shook them then lowered them to dry them on my dress but Carla stopped me because she didn't want anything to stain the bathing suit of a dress she had me wearing. She hugged me and then I stepped out.

"I'll be waiting right here for you," she said. Gaining a little more confidence from knowing Carla was waiting for me I walked to the front door and was greeted by who I presumed to be the butler. I know the home was immaculate but because I was so focused on not messing the situation up I don't really remember what I saw upon entering the colossal dwelling place of Mr. Carl Levy.

I was lead to some sort of sitting room with double doors and told to make myself comfortable and eat and drink whatever I liked. There was a small spread laid out on a side table that looked to be carved gold. On it were finger sandwiches, chocolates, chocolate strawberries, and bottles of champagne. I helped myself to two chocolate strawberries to ease my growling and unsettled stomach, figuring they were the least offensive breath wise.

About ten minutes later the double doors opened and in walked a forty-something suave-looking man that was gorgeous and had the body of an athlete. He had dark hair and piercing dark eyes that seemed as though they could cut you. He donned dark slacks and bare feet pampered by very expensive looking loafers. He wore an off-white shirt of some luxurious looking material and left several buttons undone making his smooth, chiseled chest visible.

He had a cigar in one hand and his other hand gently held a glass half filled with what appeared to be some kind of liquor. Right behind him was a beautiful woman that looked to be in her twenties that asked if he was okay and whether he needed anything else. He looked at her and told her she could go. She gave me a different kind of look. I couldn't make out what it was. I didn't think it was jealousy but more of a "What are you doing here?" type look. I don't know. Maybe it was just me.

When the woman left Mr. Levy walked over to the bar in the room and asked me if I wanted a drink. Just before I was about to decline I remembered what Carla said and agreed to have one. He paused for a moment and during that silence I realized he was waiting for me to tell him what I wanted. I suppose he sensed my inexperience at that time then offered me a glass of champagne. Before the word champagne was completely off his lips I responded eagerly-too eagerly that I'd love a glass. Inside I felt like an idiot and even deeper than that I was upset with Carla for not preparing me with the name of a drink.

By this point I was ashamed that my nervousness revealed itself and I could feel my legs trembling as I waited for Mr. Levy to hand me my glass. I took a tiny sip of the champagne and didn't like it but I eventually almost finished it as not to offend my host.

"Carla spoke so highly of you to Adam," he sad. "After hearing so much about you I just had to meet the beautiful and talented Diane Frazier. Well, one thing's for sure, I definitely like what I see," he said holding my hand high in his, and slowly turning me around in a circle to take me in with his eyes. Overwhelmingly taken over by nervousness and the fact that I had very little clothes on I gently tremble all over. Afterward we both took a seat and the meeting finally got under way.

"I guess you know who I am and that I have the power to make things happen. I can make dreams come true and I can be someone's worst nightmare. It all depends on how I'm treated and if those I help are gracious enough to help me should I need assistance."

"You need help? What on earth do you need help with?" I thought to myself as I looked around the spacious, luxurious room for emphasis.

Laughing at the expression on my face, Mr. Levy looked at me and said, "Every now and then I need little favors. Nothing one can't handle." Half satisfied with his response I nodded.

"So you want to sing. Let me hear something," he said positioning himself on the couch.

"What would you like to hear?"

"Whatever you choose my darling".

For a moment, I racked my brain for just the right song. I silently reprimanded myself for spending too much time primping for the meeting and no time choosing a song. Just then I remembered that Carla told me to just be myself so I decided to sing the song I chose for the contest. Upon finishing the song, Mr. Levy stood holding his cigar between his fingers and praised me. I blushed like a girl getting praised by the teacher she has a crush on. The both of us still standing, Mr. Levy stepped over to me and put his arm around my shoulders and told me that I was going to be a wealthy woman because of my voice.

Suddenly, in a slick move he moved to stand behind me and put both of his hands on my bare shoulders surprising me. I shivered from the coldness of the hand that held his drink and nervously allowed him to massage my shoulders, telling myself to relax and go with the flow. Although all kinds of alarms were ablaze in my mind, I allowed Carla's advice to overshadow my intuition, and slowly let down my shoulders allowing Mr. Levy's hands to move up to my neck. Shortly thereafter he lead me back to the couch he was sitting on and told me how beautifully dark my skin was. Almost in the same breath he offered me another drink and like the star pupil of Carla that I was I accepted it.

I took small sips. Then feeling brave gulped it down emptying the glass. I placed the glass on the granite coffee table and allowed my neck and shoulders to slowly melt under his hands that had been kneading me the whole time. Out of nowhere, I felt the warmth of his breath on my neck and I tensed back up pulling away from him and sat straight up on the couch.

Not missing a beat Mr. Levy said, "I have big plans for you. In no time you're going to be the next big thing out of L.A." "I'm going to get in contact with my people and put them to work immediately."

Forgetting about all that had just happened I said, "Oh thank you! Thank you!" as I jumped up and down like an excited child.

"I'll be in contact with you in a day or two. You've got a bright future ahead of you young lady," he said standing up to guide me to the double doors. As we walked his hand lightly touched me too low on the lowest part of my back. It was so low that I felt I was being violated in some way but I didn't say anything because I didn't want to offend him or accuse him of something he probably didn't mean or even realized that he did. When we reached the front door the butler opened it and standing just inside of it Mr. Levy bent down kissing me on the cheek daringly close to the corner of my mouth, and lingered there for a moment. Feeling awkward and turned on at the same time my heart rate began to race just as he straightened up and stepped away from me.

"Goodbye Diane."

"Good bye Mr. Levy and thank you." Hearing the door shut behind me I walked a little faster and fought to hide a huge, cheesy grin. Safely inside the limo I turned toward Carla and screamed in delight.

"I guess that means things went well in there?" she asked excitedly.

"Oh yeah girl, everything went well! We talked, I accepted a drink when he asked, I sang, and that was that!" Carla's eyes made her look like she was expecting more or knew more happened, but she didn't push it.

"Guess what? This means you can move out of Marlene House asap! You know I'll help you," she said.

"I don't feel like going back there right now even though I'd like to rub my pending success in her face. I'll go back when we originally planned.

"It's up to you but I'd want to get from under Marlene's roof as soon as I could. I know I couldn't wait," she said with attitude. On the ride back to Carla's house many thoughts were swirling through my head. I thought about home and how I probably wasn't going to be seeing my family for a very long time. For the first time in my life I was finally on my way to do what I always wanted to do with my life and I wasn't as happy as I wanted to be. As I thought I would be.

It was because of my parents. Sorrowfully I felt like I may not he able to trust Sharon either with her newfound relationship with God. Soon she'd be the one preaching to me like Marlene was doing. I wished I could still say I had a confidant in my sister. I concluded that I wouldn't write her off completely- yet. I figured I'd write to her and she could tell mom and dad how I'm doing or they can find out how I'm doing when they hear me on the radio and see me on television.

At least I had Carla. I knew she wouldn't let me down. She's done more for me in a couple weeks of knowing her than my own parents have done for me in my entire lifetime. At that moment I decided Carla was my family. Who needed parents like the ones I had when I had friends that really cared for me like Carla?

"Why you so quiet?" Carla asked interrupting my thoughts.

"Sorry, I was just thinking about how I have to make a few changes in my life to make it work better for me. I need to get all of the negative people out and surround myself with positivity because I'm not about to be walking around not enjoying my success just because of a few negative attitudes," I said.

"I heard that sista!" Carla said as we high fived each other. Walking into the condo girls asked me how I did and when I told them they welcomed me to my new home and congratulated me. I thought it was nice that Carla and everyone else expected me to live there but as soon as I could afford to move I was leaving. I wanted my own space and my own things. I went from living in my parent's home to moving into Marlene House, to moving into Carla's condo that she shared with three other girls. Now that I was going to be living with Carla I'd have to share a room with her.

After I changed into sweatpants and a tee shirt we went downstairs for a snack.

"So you're the new girl huh?" a pretty Asian girl said.

"Yeah that's me," I said chewing a piece of lunchmeat.

"What do you do?" she asked.

"Oh, I sing. Carl's gonna hook me up with a singing contract," I said between bites.

"Yeah. Carl's gonna hook you up with a lot of other things too," she said turning to walk away."

"Shut up Tina," a redhead said walking into the room.

"I'm telling the truth and you know it," Tina said whipping her head around to face the other girl. "I wish you the best though," then Tina left the kitchen.

"What did she mean by that?" I asked Carla who had busied herself with stirring a pitcher of Kool-Aid.

"She doesn't mean anything. Tina's probably just jealous because she hasn't had a photo shoot in three weeks. She runs her mouth too much and when your words catch up with you, you have to suffer the consequences."

"So, Tina said something she shouldn't have and as a punishment she can't work?"

"You got it. We have certain rules we have to abide by when we sign a contract with Carl. If you breach the contract you're out, but because Carl doesn't want to see anyone out on the streets or their career ruined, he has other ways for us to make up for whatever it is," she said tasting Kool-Aid from the ladle she held.

"Is that normal? Is that a standard contract? Is that even legal? Is that the same kind of contract Mr. Levy is going to give me?" I asked.

"Why wouldn't he? It's the same contract all of us have. Why would yours be any different?" And to answer your other questions, it's normal and yes it's legal and binding," she said flurrying around the kitchen making a sandwich.

"I didn't mean it like that and I didn't mean for you to take it personally either. I just don't have any other offers to compare it to."

"Oh, so you're trying to turn this around on me!" she snapped. "I bend over backward so you can have an opportunity to make a name for yourself out here and now you're getting on me for forgetting one little thing- excuse me! Next time I'll keep a checklist of every last bit of information about something before I come to you so I won't be confronted like this!" she said slamming the refrigerator door causing magnets to fall to the floor.

Gaining confidence to backtalk the one person I had in my corner I said, "Carla I don't know what you heard because that's not what I said! You're taking what I said totally the wrong way and you're all upset for nothing! I'm not apologizing for what I said because you didn't tell me about the contract! How did you expect me to react when I found out about the contract? Is that why you didn't tell me?"

"I didn't say anything about the contract because I didn't think it mattered at the time."

"Well, just so you know it did matter," I said blowing by Carla and a girl named Sanya. I bounded up the stairs feeling confused. Once I reached my shared room with Carla I slammed the door behind me, and pressed my back against it and stood there.

"Please don't let Marlene be right about Carla. I still don't believe

Marlene but Carla's not telling me about being punished and not being able to work if I say the wrong things doesn't sound right, but I don't have anywhere else to go. Marlene is wrong, she was lying. Yeah, Carla has my best interest at heart and if she, Tina, Sanya, and Allison all have the same contract it can't be all that bad. Yeah, it can't be all that bad. All contracts have do's and don'ts and the one I'm going to sign is no different."

Taking a deep breath to further calm myself I said, *"I want this. This is what I came to California for. I'm not backing down because everything isn't perfect. Nothing is ever perfect."*

I turned around and opened the door prepared to apologize to Carla and close the tiny rift that was created by our outbursts. Heading downstairs I slowed up when I heard Sanya and Tina talking in the kitchen.

"Well, I think you did the right thing. I mean, the girl needs to know what she's getting into and…"

"Hey guys," I said stepping into the kitchen hoping they'd level with me, but no such luck. They scattered at the sight of me. Looking for Carla so we could talk about what happened, I used the opportunity to check out my temporary home. The kitchen was large, but not the size of Marlene's. There were modern appliances everywhere and a table that looked like a booth at a restaurant to accommodate all the girls.

Off the kitchen, near the table was a short hall that lead to a laundry room and a powder room. Exiting the kitchen through the main way was a larger hall that lead to the foyer and front door if you turned right. Straight ahead was a sunken den that flowed into a dining room that had sliding doors leading to a deck that held a grill, table, chairs, portable bar, and a hot tub.

Off of the dining room was a room that served as an office and library. You could get upstairs the main way or by a set of stairs leading from the office. Upstairs were bathrooms and bedrooms. All in all I liked it but I was still planning to move as soon as I started making money.

Walking back around to take another look at the deck I caught a glimpse of Carla coming down the back stairs into the library so I took a detour to talk to her.

"Hey," I said.

"Hey."

"Listen, I …" We both said at the same time and laughed. I gestured that she could go first then she said the same thing to me then I insisted.

"Carla, you go first because I wouldn't even be here if it wasn't for you."

"You know, you're right, I should've told you about the contract. I didn't tell you because...... huhhh, I didn't tell you because I didn't know if you'd be cool with meeting Carl if you knew he treats us like his own personal property. I didn't tell you because I wanted you to come here so I could have a friend and since I knew how bad you want to make it and Carl can make that happen, I didn't tell you," she said looking away taking a deep breath, and exhaling.

I believed her. I suppose I wouldn't have said anything about it either. But what kind of friend would I be to do that? I decided to drop it and move on to other more important things. Carla agreed and we went out back on the deck to talk.

"So are we friends again?" Carla asked holding her arms open for a hug. I leaned in and hugged her back. I learned that I was the only one there that sang or wanted to sing professionally. Tina was a model, Sanya was an actress and dancer, and Allison was an actress. We talked until the sun went down then headed inside for bed.

I was a little hurt because Carla tried to trick me. I say tried to trick me because it's not like I actually signed something not knowing what I was getting into. For a second I thought about going upstairs to get my things then call a cab to take me back to Marlene House. In the very next second I decided I wouldn't dare go back there without being able to tell Marlene that I made it and that Carla isn't who she said she is for sure. For sure. Does that mean I have little bit of doubt when it comes to Carla? I don't know. I'll never admit it.

CHAPTER 13

Diane

You're going to feel my pain

The next morning around ten the phone rang and someone downstairs yelled for me to pick up the line. After being on the phone a few minutes I hung up smiling, then Carla walked into the room carrying a bag of clothes that needed to be dry cleaned and asked me if that was "the" call. I told her it was.

"Well, what did she say?" she asked.

"Well, that was Mr. Levy. He said he'll send someone over later today with a contract for me to sign then once he has it he can get the ball rolling. Actually, I'm scheduled to begin rehearsing with a new group called Classique on Saturday. I'll start off in this group then he said in no time I'll have my own solo career."

"Wow," Carla said, "Carl just about never makes his own calls. Usually, you only speak to Carl at the first meeting then whenever he calls you for his favors," she said. "I wonder why he called you?" She asked out loud dwelling on what I thought was an unimportant issue.

"Okay, I'm getting ready to drop these things off at the cleaners," she said grabbing her keys from the dresser, "you wanna come?"

"Uh, no thanks, I'm gonna stay and straighten up in here now that my bed has arrived," I said.

"Okay, see you when I get back."

A few hours later there was a knock at the door. Tina answered it and called me to the foyer. A woman stood there dressed very business-like carrying a briefcase. She asked if we could go somewhere private to discuss the contract. I nodded and lead her to the office. Shutting the door behind her I motioned that we could sit on the couch.

After ten minutes passed the contract was signed and Mr. Levy's

115

assistant was on her way. Feeling good about my future I walked back to the office to get some paper so I could write to Sharon and tell her the good news. I like to wait until I know for sure that whatever I'm doing is a sure thing. I don't like having to explain why something didn't happen the way I planned it.

When Saturday rolled around I drove to the rehearsal. I was signed as the fourth member of a female r&b group called Classique. They were cool, had a cool sound and I could really groove with them. I could tell I was a perfect fit. I could also tell that the girls felt the same way. Soon I was rehearsing everyday and Carla was out most days on the set of the new movie she was casted for. We were both working very hard and hardly saw each other.

Classique was finally told that we'd be going on the road for six months. We sang at lots of clubs and different venues in L.A. and neighboring cities and received rave reviews. I was excited but wasn't sure what our schedule would be like. When I found out a few weeks later I wrote to Sharon telling her that I'd send her a ticket as soon as they became available.

Just before I sent the letter out I received a response from my first letter to her. She asked all the regular questions but also said that mom and dad ask and talk about me all the time and that they miss me. Well, they should've thought about all that before they pushed me away from them. I really didn't want to hear anything about my parents except for their well being. Other than that I didn't want anything to do with them so I didn't even acknowledge that Sharon mentioned them in her letter.

Just before we headed out for our tour around the country, I received a letter from Sharon stating that I didn't have to send tickets because she'd already purchased front row tickets for one of our New York shows. At the time I didn't think anything of the fact that the word tickets means more than one ticket, so when we got to New York after three months of touring I was surprised to see Sharon and my parents grinning in the front row.

Despite seeing my sister and looking forward to seeing her beforehand, the sight of my parents caused my stomach to burn. I had no plans to forgive them. They were going to pay for making my life miserable and I wanted to make theirs just as miserable if not more for not supporting me, then trying to instill the fear of failing in me.

The whole time I was on stage their eyes were glued to me. I was glad I had on the shortest, tightest dress out of all the girls. I made sure I shook my behind and waved my arms more dramatically than need be. I imagined they were appalled at how I was dressed and flaunting my body.

I wanted them to hate it and then let the inability to not tell me what to do eat away at them. I wanted to tell Sharon that I had a surprise for her in my last letter but I decided on telling her in person that I arranged for her to come backstage to meet the girls and hang out in our dressing room.

I didn't know how she'd react to everything as a whole because of her knew found beliefs but I knew she'd be happy to see me and be my biggest fan. Toward the end of the show, I stepped away from my place with the other girls and sang a duet with the lead singer. I saw my family's eyes grow big with surprise and I could see pride in them. I sang hard and loud for Sharon to make her proud and at my parents as if to say "in your face."

Just as the song ended I saw tears on Sharon and my mom's faces. My dad had a look of awe. I felt something pulling in my chest but I willed it away. There was no way I was going to share a tender moment with my parents especially since they came to my concert uninvited. As we stood waiting for our names to be announced by Needra, the leader of our group, I became enraged at Sharon for being sneaky and bringing my parents when she knew full well that I didn't want to see them. I had no desire to share any of this experience with them.

Our hands clasped together and raised we took a bow and then another and exited the stage. I reminded one of the guys in the back that he was to let my sister in and I headed toward my dressing room. Moments later I heard my name called and turned to see that it was Sharon then I saw her turn and motion to someone or more like it, to two someones. My parents were right behind her.

"I'm only letting you in Sharon," I said as the three of them drew closer to me standing in the doorway.

"Diane, how could you?" She asked in surprise. "They're our parents. They want to see you. They want to talk to you," she pleaded.

"Not today," I said firmly. I saw my mom pat Sharon on her shoulder and Sharon turned her ear to her. It was becoming crowded back there so I read my mom's lips.

She said, "That's okay honey. You go on ahead, we'll be waiting in the car." Sharon looked at me and pleaded with her eyes one final time but I looked away. Finally, I closed the door behind Sharon and offered her a seat after we hugged.

"I'm not gonna go there with you, but you know you were wrong. That's all I have to say," she said trying on the heels I kicked off as soon as I got to the dressing room. Ignoring what she said I told her that she looked good and how happy I was to see her. We talked as I changed and packed my bags. We agreed to hang out the last night of Classique's visit to New York, and I couldn't wait.

I truly wanted to hang out right then and there but I was tired and had an exhausting day ahead of me because we had three different shows to do in the city. The last night, the third night, we only had one and it was earlier than all the others. I hoped to get back to the hotel, shower, get some rest, then meet up with Sharon.

"You only have two parents Diane," she said.

"No, really? I thought I just appeared out of nowhere or something," I joked.

"No, I'm serious. I know you hate them and you want to get back at them. I want you to know that they really wanted to see you tonight. They were so happy when I told them I had front row tickets. Mom cried and was so excited that she went out and got her hair and nails done and bought a new outfit. They're both very proud of you."

Unmoved by her revelation I didn't acknowledge what she said as she walked toward the door. Instead of responding I hugged her and kissed her cheek and told her to drive safely and that I'd call her in two days to let her know where we could meet.

Just before she started to walk off she turned and said, "Don't let unforgiveness eat away at you. Don't be bitter because you'll be the one paying for it spiritually, physically, and emotionally. You'll be worse off than mom and dad will ever be if you keep punishing them." After that she walked off. I stood in the door watching her until she disappeared around a corner. Sharon was not going to scare me or think me into talking to my parents.

The next two days flew by and the last show was over. I walked into my group's double room and fell backwards on the bed, my shoes flying off my feet. I contacted Sharon early that morning to discuss where we'd meet and what we'd do. Before we hung up silly Sharon made yet another attempt for me to have some kind of contact with my parents, by asking me to meet with them before the tour left New York.

"Sharon, I don't need you to be a mediator between me, mom, and dad. When I'm ready to write to them, meet with them, or call them I'll do it. It'll be when I'm good and ready and on my terms. I don't have anything else to say about this subject. Please just go back to being the sister that I can laugh and have fun with because you're about to get on my last nerve with all this," I said dismissing the topic.

"Okay, okay. I admit I've been a little pushy so I'll leave you alone...

for now," she added quickly. We both laughed because we knew that for now to Sharon meant no more than a week.

In the early evening, after my last New York show, Sharon and I met up in the lobby of my hotel. It was just like Sharon to not have me go anywhere to meet her. I guess she was determined to always be protective of me. It's cool though. At least I know she'll always have my back.

❧

Laughter filled the air of the outdoor restaurant as we followed the hostess to our table by the water. The lights on the building we were eating behind as well as the others across the water made everything so beautiful. Their reflection danced on the gently moving water creating images I tried to figure out.

It was late September, 1975, and we were blessed with a very warm day. Throughout dinner we talked and laughed, then laughed until we cried. Most of the conversation was about our lives, hopes, and dreams, and our plans for the future. I found out that Sharon had been dating a guy she met the first day she moved into her new place. She talked about how sweet he is and how he does everything for her. She mentioned that he's saved and is actually the reason why she became saved.

"When he introduced himself to me outside the building that I worked in I could tell there was something different about him. He was different from all the guys I've dated and even encounter on a daily basis for one reason or another. We talked for about fifteen minutes and he asked me to dinner that night. I said yes and he picked me up at my apartment later that evening. On the way he talked about his church and asked me about my church background, but I was a little embarrassed to tell him that I grew up not going to church and that I hadn't been as an adult except for weddings, funerals, and baby dedications.

I expected him to laugh at me but he didn't. Instead he invited me to his church that upcoming Sunday. The first time at his church was interesting and informative. I obtained some knowledge about myself, God's character, and life, and I wanted more so I continued to go. After three months passed I decided to get saved, I mean give my life to God."

I think I must've shown disinterest on my face because the next thing she said was, "Oh, I'm sorry, I didn't mean to go on like that."

"No, that's alright," I lied, not wanting her to know that in my mind I saw myself rolling my eyes at every word she said. After dinner we saw a new movie called "Three Days of Condor". Robert Redford and Faye

Dunaway were in it. I gave it two thumbs up. Afterward we decided to walk around the city and enjoy the sights. The next thing we knew it was about eleven at night and Sharon had to leave. She'd taken a few days off from work to spend with me, mom, and dad. But now her mini vacation was over.

Standing on the stairs of my hotel we said our goodbyes and Sharon left. I was sad seeing Sharon go because to me she was the only real family I had, the only person I could talk to. Not only that, but I didn't know when I'd get to see her again or get a letter from her since I'd just found out we were going on an international tour for almost a whole year after returning to L.A. for a short time.

That night lying in the bed next to one of my group members I lay awake looking into the darkness. Every time I closed my eyes to sleep I saw my family as they were at the concert side by side in the front row. Left to right before me. Sharon. Mom. Dad. Something in my chest kept pulling, kept pushing but my memories kept me strong against the force that was trying to break me, weaken me.

The nights I cried myself to sleep because I was so hurt, and unhappy, and miserable that I couldn't be myself in my own house hurt me deeply and my parents were the source of that hurt. No, they wouldn't hear from me for a long, long time.

For the next three months we toured up and down the east coast then ended the tour where it began in L.A. We were a huge success. Our songs were being played on the radio and my dreams were coming true. I thought back to my last day of class at Vernard Community College and how I wanted to hear my voice on the radio. Even though my voice was blended with three others I still made it and if everything worked out the way Carl said it would, I'd be hearing my own voice soon enough.

Chapter 14

Diane

Get me outta here!

Our travels overseas were both memorable and a blur. They were memorable because of the beautiful places we sang in, the beautiful scenery, and most of all because of all the love showered on us by our fans. We really didn't want to leave but on the other hand we were exhausted and homesick. Traveling and sightseeing when we had small windows of time for fun added to our exhaustion because we had to squeeze everything into one to two days then pack up and catch a plane back to L.A.

Eight months later we returned home learned women. We felt like pros and no one could tell us anything. I was anxious to get back to my own bed that I didn't have to share with anyone and I wondered how many letters from Sharon I had waiting for me. I wondered how Carla was doing.

Opening the front door and catching a quick glance of whatever was in my path on my way up the stairs I continued on. I pushed open the bedroom door to find the room in complete chaos. It was in total disarray. Clothes were strewn everywhere. They were on the floor, hanging off the doorknobs, the curtains, the dresser, the television, everywhere.

Carla's bed wasn't made and although mine was made before I left to tour, it looked like someone had just jumped out of it. I mustered up some strength after carrying up my luggage to do a powerful sweep of my bed and pushed everything off of it in one swoosh. I of course had no idea where Carla was and it appeared that I was the only one home.

I surveyed the room and began picking up things and turning things over for clues as to where Carla was or at least what happened to the room while I was away. I checked Carla's closet and her luggage was gone so that meant she was out of town. Being an actress shooting a movie she could be anywhere in the world so I left it at that.

That was when I sat down on the edge of my bed nearest the nightstand Carla and I shared between our beds and saw Carla's handwriting sprawled across a sheet of memo paper. It was dated the day before and had an address in Malibu written on it. Underneath was written *2 nights plus.*

I wondered what that could mean and continued staring at the piece of paper as though it would tell me. Annoyed at the condition of the room I stood up to put it in order. About an hour later I folded my blanket over my pillow and ran my hand over the top of the blanket to smooth everything out. I walked downstairs and plopped down on the couch after turning the television on, then the phone rang.

It was Mr. Levy congratulating me for a job well done while on tour. On a few different occasions I took Needra's place as lead singer because she was ill and couldn't perform. She kept coming down with colds that affected her lungs and breathing. I think she had bronchitis and laryngitis so her voice was no good for a while.

I wasn't nervous at all about taking the stage front and center. I did my thing and kept it moving, waiting for the next opportunity to take Needra's place again. Not that I was out to take her place but I wanted to show everyone that it was no sweat taking the lead. There were times I pictured myself in the lead position of Classique and my fantasy actually came true.

"Thank you Mr. Levy. It really means a lot to me to know that you were pleased with my performance on tour. I hope I have more opportunities to show you that I'm an asset to Berdynu Records," I said as syrupy sweet as I could, but I meant it.

"Now that's what I like to hear. I like your go getter attitude. I need more girls like you. Always remember what I told you about a solo career. I see it in the horizon for you. If you keep it up you'll be where you want to be in no time," he said encouragingly.

"Thank you Mr. Levy".

"Listen, call me Carl. You're the only one of my girls that calls me Mr. Levy. I figured you'd start calling me Carl after hanging around the rest of the girls, but I see you need an invitation," he said in a joking manner. "Alright, time to get serious again," he said, the laughter no longer in his voice. "If you're as serious as you say you are, I mean really serious about taking your career to another level you've got to start thinking about what you're willing to give, how much of yourself you're willing to give to stop dreaming your dream and live it."

Getting excited about what his next words would be I stood up and paced the floor carrying the phone around with me. "Oh yes Mr. .... I mean Carl, I'm dedicated and serious about this. I've never wanted anything more in my life," I said.

"Excellent, I see I'm not going to have a hard time with you. You know what you want and have the attitude it takes to get it," he said speaking louder. "With that understood, I need a favor from you."

"From me? Sure, anything for you Carl."

"See, I knew I was going to like you when I first met you," he said. "I'm having a lavish get together for some friends of mine this weekend and I want you to be present should any of them need any assistance with anything while they're there. I want you to make them feel comfortable and whatever else may come to mind."

"Oh, of course," I said, "I'm flattered that you'd even want me to come," I said like an attention starved teenager. I hated my response right after I said it although I meant it. "What should I wear?"

"You know what? I'd really like to see you in the dress you wore when we first met," he said with a hint of something in his voice that I couldn't identify. "That or something like it. You looked quite stunning in it," he said with the same mystery in his voice.

"Alright, I'll wear the dress just for you," I said trying to return what I thought was a flirty statement.

"I can't wait," he said. "I'll have one of my assistants call with the time a car will arrive to pick you up."

"Okay, I'll be waiting and I look forward to seeing you and helping you out," I said.

"Remember, always keep your eyes on the prize," then he hung up.

Sitting there on the couch I thought about my conversation with Carl. He was kind of mysterious in the way he spoke and I liked that. However, I wasn't really pleased with the fact that he wanted me to wear the dress that I balled up and threw in the bottom of my closet as soon as I took it off. I hated that thing although it brought me good luck. I mean, I wore it on the most important day of my life but that's as sentimental as I was going to get over it.

Opening the closet door and walking inside I looked down at the dress on the floor and rolled my eyes. "Guess I have to take a trip to the dry cleaners," I said grabbing my purse and keys and heading downstairs. As I was reaching for the doorknob it turned and the door opened. It was Tina, Sanya, and Allison. They filed in the house one after the other carrying a suitcase or overnight bag.

"Wow, everyone takes a vacation at the same time in this house?" I asked laughing.

"It depends on what you call a vacation," Tina said in her loaded response way.

"Shut up," one of the girls said as I closed the door behind me.

While I was turning my key to lock the door I heard Tina's voice through it. "You girls need to stop acting like this. You know this isn't right and someone needs to tell her. She's walking around thinking everything is cool. I really don't think she knows what she's in for." After that I didn't hear anything else. Their voices sounded further away. I imagined them taking their bags upstairs.

By now I was truly curious about what my housemates were talking about. I don't know what went on while I was gone but I had the feeling Allison, Tina, and Sanya were all away together, which is no big deal. Friends go on vacation all the time, but the remark Tina made about what my idea of a vacation was and me needing to know what I'm in for had me a little worried.

I had to figure out a way to have a private conversation with Tina, because at that moment I realized that Tina and I were never in a room by ourselves. If the two of us were alone either Sanya, Allison, or even Carla popped up out of nowhere and Tina's demeanor would change. She'd go from seeming like she wanted to talk to being distant.

"*Shut up,*" I said ordering the voice in my head that told me Marlene was right about Carla. "*Diane here you go thinking about what Marlene said and you know good and well that if it was true you would've known it by now. Stop acting like this,*" I scolded myself. With that I dismissed the thought and drove away.

CHAPTER 15

Diane

A place of my own

One of the things I wanted to do as soon as I got home from touring was look for my own place. I wanted to be able to walk through my home without seeing other people and their guests there. I wanted my refrigerator stocked with only the things I liked and wanted and peace and quiet among other things. Sometimes Tina, Allison, and Sanya could get loud when they invited people over. I couldn't wait to move.

On my way home I passed a house for sale and jotted down the name of the realtor whose information was on the for sale sign. Once home, I called the agent and explained what I was looking for. I set up an appointment for the next day with a woman named Deidra Thomas. I hoped she could find what I was looking for.

When I got home everyone was doing their own thing so I went to my room to do the same. I had a lot on my plate but had two weeks to relax before my life became hectic again. After that Classique would be in the studio making music. Then we had dance rehearsals to attend. In addition to that lots of shows were scheduled for months, so I knew I had to utilize my time off wisely.

The next day I hoped for the opportunity to talk to Tina privately, but the chance never came. Sometimes I wished I could just tap into her thoughts and get whatever information I needed. She knew something I needed to know, but what would I do with it? Despite the situation at home I was determined to enjoy the time spent with the real estate agent. She told me to meet her at the agency then we'd leave in her car to see some properties for sale.

I entered the building full of excitement and told the receptionist that I had an appointment with an agent named Deidra Thomas. She nodded and picked up her phone to place a call. When she hung up about a minute later she said someone would be out to help me. Looking down into my purse for a moment to search for a mint I suddenly saw a black pair of men's dress shoes on the floor before me. I followed the rest of the man from his feet to his handsome face.

"Good morning," his mouth opened and said, "My name is Gregory Williams. I presume you're Ms. Frazier."

"Yes, but you can call me Diane," I said totally into him.

"Thank you Diane. Are ready to go?" He asked.

"Uh, yes, but I thought I was meeting with Deidra Thomas."

"I apologize for that. She's unable to meet with you but since my schedule is free I'm available to show you the properties she planned to take you to see. So, are you ready to hit the road?"

"Sure, where are we going first?" I asked not caring the least bit that Deidra Thomas was unable to see me. In his car I relaxed as much as I could for a girl who was knocked off balance by such a good looking man. Every now and then I felt him glance at me and a couple times I was sure he was about to say something but changed his mind. I was flattered that he was attracted to me because he could easily have any woman he wanted.

We drove on making small talk and me talking about my music career. Gregory showed me house after house, and then he began showing me condos which is what I said I wanted in the first place. Finally we came to a very tall building of condos. So far so good. I liked what I saw. Everything about the building was me. It felt like me. Sensing that I was really digging everything, he held his hand up waiting for me to give him a high five and we took the elevator to the seventh floor. Once the elevator doors opened Gregory handed me a key with a tag on it that read *seven-hundred twenty two.*

I took it, walked to the door with seven-hundred twenty two on it, and turned the key. Once inside I knew I'd found my new home. The carpet and wood flooring, the space, the kitchen, the windows, and the breathtaking view...

"I'll take it," I said after walking through every room in a rush as Gregory pointed out different highlights of the dwelling.

"You sure?" he asked looking at me.

"Yes," I said returning his look that asked, "Are you sure you don't want to take more time to think about this?" with an "I don't know how you make a living asking questions like that" look of my own.

"Okay then," he said brightening up and pulling documents from a folder. "Let me get some information from you and we'll get the process started."

"I want to do whatever needs to be done in order to move in within the next week," I said meaning business.

"Listen," he said, "I don't want to offend you in any way but God had us meet for a reason." I rolled my eyes and sucked my teeth taking in and releasing an exasperated breath of air. "Now I know you made an appointment with Deidra Thomas but at the last minute she couldn't meet with you after having a clear schedule and at the last minute all of my appointments called to cancel or reschedule."

Not sure where he was going with this I asked, "So what does this have to do with me?" My anger was rising.

"It has everything to do with you. God wanted us to meet and I'm going to tell you why," he said. "From the moment I turned the corner from my office and saw you the Holy Spirit has been speaking to me about you and showing me things about you." I stood there in a defiant stance. "He says you ran away from home to pursue a dream- to sing. Your parents are against it. He says you've experienced some success but your heart is hardened. You don't have a relationship with Him. He wants you to make things right with your parents. You need to talk to them and forgive them. You're headed in a direction He never planned for you to travel. You look at others and see their success but God says their reward is here on this earth, because they're living for themselves and have no regard for Him and the purpose for which He created them, nor the life that comes after this one. He says He blessed you with gifts and talents to be faithful with them. You're in bondage and don't even know it. In the Spirit I see ropes wrapped around you that say unforgiveness and strife. He says He sent His Son Jesus to set the captives free. He says you are stubborn. He sent two others before me to warn you but there will be no more after me if you continue to ignore Him. He says He created you for a beautiful purpose and that you are to use your voice for the good of the Kingdom, for His glory. He says your life will overflow with the joy, peace, and fulfillment that you're seeking when you turn to Him. He's given you all the resources you need in order to fulfill your purpose on this earth. He loves you Diane. That's what He's saying right now. He's telling me to tell you that He loves you. He's saying I love you daughter. Sing for Me."

My eyes clouded over and some tears fell.

"See, you know everything that I've said is true. You know there's no way I could've known all those things about you. I don't know you. I've never seen you and I don't know anything about your music although I do remember seeing your group on a billboard once, but that's it. God is trying to get through to you Diane. If you continue to ignore Him I don't know what may happen. You see God is a gentleman. He's not going to force you to do anything. He won't push Himself on you. He just won't do it. You need God's guidance. Allow yourself to be drawn in by the Holy Spirit. His Holy Spirit will teach you and will show you who you are in Christ Jesus and exactly what your purpose on this earth is. Let Him love you and guide you in the direction He planned for you to go. I'm sorry but you're not going to be happy until you acknowledge that you need Him. Bow down and humble yourself before Him and allow Him into your heart. He says you're going to be carrying a heavy load, much heavier than anything you've ever experienced if you continue to ignore Him. He says His burden is light and His yoke is easy. He'll fill you with His Holy Spirit and you'll be filled will power. You'll be able to hear the voice of the Holy Spirit like I can. He's the one that told me all about – "

"All about me and *my* business!" I said cutting him off. "Why did you have to come here?!" I screamed like a lunatic. "My life was going fine until you opened your mouth! Why couldn't you just do your job and show me this place and keep your mouth shut!" I was furious and my face was wet with tears and wetness was trickling from my nostrils and spittle shot from my mouth as I yelled.

"I can't keep my mouth shut Diane. I must obey God. I must do and say what His Spirit tells me and go where His spirit tells me. I'd be disobeying God if I didn't share those things with you," he said closing the gap between us. God doesn't want to be ignored just like you or I or anyone else doesn't like it. I love to hear the voice of the Holy Spirit. I know I'm in tune and connected to the Source. That inner witness is amazing," he said as his sincere belief blossomed on his face.

I knew he had total confidence in what he believed and he was trying to get me to feel the same way. I looked down and saw that both our hands were on the kitchen counter and almost touched. I was secretly embarrassed for thinking that he was struggling to come up with right words to ask me out on a date earlier. The whole time he wanted to tell me what he claims the Holy Spirit was telling him about me. How foolish of me to think that my journey to stardom was going to be easy and filled with well-wishers.

Instead it was littered with naysayers and negativity, and a God that didn't want me to succeed. Who would sing for God's benefit? It surely wouldn't benefit me and my career, so who? Why? What's so wrong with me singing? The one thing in life that I want to do so badly seemed to be the worst thing, the bane of my existence.

"Diane, you need to make a choice. Either you're going to turn to God or turn your back. God loves you Diane and He wants the best of life for you. Try Him and I know you won't be disappointed."

"Gregory, all that sounds fine and good," I said feeling wounded and weary, "but this is my life. When I'm ready to make that change I will. Until then I'm not thinking about that. I don't even know what I really think about God. Maybe the Holy Spirit told you all those things about me or maybe not. I don't know. I've been doing fine without Him for nineteen years so why would I change anything if nothing's wrong? Neither of my parents went to church when I was growing up so if they did it I can do it too. My sister says they're going now – not that I care but I can see myself slowing down later in life and seeing what all this God stuff is about. Quite frankly I'm tired of hearing about it. Now, getting back to why we're here, I like everything about this place. I need you to stop being the bearer of bad news for a few minutes and be my real estate agent," I said dismissing the conversation he'd started.

"Don't worry I'm not going to say anything else. I did what I was supposed to do, now it's your turn to do what you know you should do. One last thing though, and I promise I won't say anything else," he said seeking permission to continue, "God won't ever turn His back on you. He'll be waiting and watching as you make mistake after mistake, for the moment you realize that you really do need Him after all."

"That may be a long wait," I said watching him thumb through sheets of paper in his briefcase.

CHAPTER 16

Diane

What's going on here?

I drove to the dry cleaners to pick up the horrid makes-me-feel-naked dress that Carl requested that I wear as I sang happily thinking about my soon to be new home. The affair was in one more day so that gave me enough time to get to the hair salon so I could be beautiful and be the eye candy Carl expected me to be.

When I got home from getting dolled up everyone was there except for Carla. I asked if anyone knew where she was and the only response I got was that she was working. Instantly my mind went back to the address on Carla's memo pad. The next morning, I received a call from Carl's office telling me what time to expect a car and to bring an overnight bag in case the party ran too late. I was actually excited about things running late and spending the night in Carl's beach house.

I was so excited. That evening around seven the doorbell rang and it was one of Carl's drivers. I walked outside carrying my overnight bag and a small purse to match my dress and slid inside the limo. My mind reflected on the look the girls gave me as I walked toward the door. Tina just shook her head and Allison and Sanya both looked at me as if to say "You aint going nowhere special," then Sanya waved goodbye to me and cracked a smile. Allison jabbed her in the side with her elbow. I was glad I was about to be out of that house I thought, as the limo cruised to Malibu.

Not that I felt that Carla had to do it, but I felt she would want to keep in touch so we could find out how the other was doing, but I hadn't heard from her and it was bothering me a little.

Of course the beach house was amazing. It was white with windows galore and seemed to be about four levels. All kinds of luxury cars were in the driveway and limos were pulling away one after the other dropping off guests. I stepped inside and searched the crowd for a familiar face. After scanning the room a second time I found Carl across the room and our eyes locked. He excused himself from the conversation he was having with a group of people and headed in my direction.

"Ah, you look lovely Diane. Just like I remember you," he said kissing me on the cheek and then leading me through the crowd with his hand on my lower back. Both men and women turned and stared at me. I felt like a precious stone being transported through a crowd of onlookers because I was to be placed on exhibit for all to adore.

Ultimately I figured they recognized me as a member of Classique. I was slowly mellowing out naturally, as I grew more comfortable with my surroundings. Then Carl and I entered a room through French doors that were being guarded by two men that looked as though they were with secret service. They both turned toward the doors, one on either side as we approached them and opened the doors wide for us.

Once inside I was taken to another place in time or at least just another place. There were colors everywhere. Flowing fabric of beautiful colors hung low from the ceiling separating sections of the room off. There were pillows of different sizes on the floor and some as big as mattresses. All the colors reminded me of Carla's room back home. The ceiling was covered with the colorful flowing fabric and it hung in such a way that it appeared as suspended ocean waves reflecting a rainbow and spread by setting sunlight.

I felt like I'd been transported to Arabia as we walked further into the fairytale-like room. There were large rectangular shaped tables that were strategically placed throughout the room into sunken areas of the floor. I noticed that those who wanted to had to step down to lounge around the tables on plush pillows. The tables were decorated with beautiful trinkets that sparkled endlessly. There were goblets and vases of different shapes, colors, and sizes on each table. I knew they were filled with the most expensive wines, champagnes, and liquors that Carl's money could buy.

There were huge platters of the most succulent, firmest, most perfect fruit, nuts, cheeses, breads, dips, and spreads for everyone to sample as they wished. Each table highlighted a different main course. I saw huge lobsters, crabs, and other seafood on one table, then bowls and bowls of pasta on another. Yet still there was another table that showcased innumerable legs of lamb, Cornish hens, steaks, and on the table I was closest to, two roasted suckling pigs.

A few moments later the lights were dimmed very low throughout the entire room then lights I thought were permanent fixtures in the ceiling slowly descended until they were about two feet above each table giving off just enough light to enable everyone to see each other and eat. A wall slowly slid away and a dj appeared with his equipment. He set the music and beautiful, seductive sounds filled every space as its heartbeat-like bass permeated through me.

I noticed that there was no dress code. Everyone came as they wanted. I saw long evening gowns and tuxedos, hip huggers, hot pants, tube tops, slicked back hair, afros, and cornrows. Every style and nationality was represented in that room.

We stopped at the table covered with what seemed like every kind of seafood imaginable and Carl helped me to my pillow seat. I quickly glanced under the table before sitting and realized that everyone was barefoot. I looked closer and saw another recessed area beneath the table where everyone kicked off their shoes. Finding a comfortable position I watched as Carl unbuttoned his suit jacket a little then he sat down beside me.

The table seated the ten of us comfortably and I observed everyone there. There were two couples at the table from what I could tell because of wedding rings and they sat next to each other. One couple looked to be together because they sat very close and the other I couldn't tell because they leaned into each other as well as the man or woman on their other side. A man at our table raised his glass for a toast to Carl. He said a lot of nice things but one of the last things was that he was thankful to Carl for giving them pleasure and beauty then I'm pretty certain he looked directly at me before taking a sip of whatever he'd poured himself.

A bolt of electricity flowed through me when he looked at me. I don't know why and it both startled and embarrassed me because I hoped he hadn't noticed. We helped ourselves to whatever we wanted. Carl took pleasure in preparing my plate with a little of everything as well as filling my glass high with a deep red wine.

We all chattered about a host of things like the celebrities in the room and other parts of the house as well as who they thought to be the wealthiest person at the table. Then the conversation turned to me after the man that gave the toast asked Carl who his beautiful friend was.

"Everyone, this is Diane," he said gesturing with his hand as though he was about to unveil something out of this world. The strange thing is that the people at the table responded as though he was. I waved and said that I was glad to be there. I turned to Carl and thanked him openly for inviting me.

"Oh you're most welcome sweetheart," he said rubbing my arm. Eventually people from our table and the other tables got up and walked away to dance, sit down in other areas of the room, or to stand with the dj and groove. On the ride over the thought came to me that Carl might want me to sing so I came prepared just in case.

After a few more minutes passed by two men and a woman entered the room each holding a platter. Carl signaled the woman over to our table. Only me, Carl, the man that toasted and the woman I thought to be his wife remained. The woman with the tray bent down revealing an assortment of pills. The pills were different sizes, shapes, and colors, but were sectioned off by color. Carl took one and swallowed it then looked at the platter, then to me, then back at the platter and handed me a tiny lavender pill. He placed it in the palm of my hand and handed me my glass from the table.

He encouraged me to take it. As I contemplated whether I should, the toaster and his wife chose theirs then the woman carrying the platter moved on to another table.

"Go ahead Diane, take it," Carl said as I looked at him with "why?" written on my face. "I'd never tell you to do something that you wouldn't benefit from in the end," he said taking my hand gently in his and raising it to my mouth. I looked over to the couple at our table and the woman held up her own little lavender pill like she was showing it off.

"Honey, it'll be fine. It'll be the nicest and smoothest ride you've ever taken." I considered what she said but I wasn't one for alcohol and I certainly wasn't in to taking pills.

"Carl why –," then I stopped talking. For a brief moment my mind went to what Carla said about not offending Carl by taking whatever he offers me. Then I thought about Tina being punished by Carl for some reason, so I took the pill. I took two big swallows of the wine and sat there. About five minutes later the man and the woman got up and walked toward a closed door then the woman kissed the man and walked away. He stood there and waited a moment then he stepped into the room and closed the door.

"Diane, he's my most distinguished guest. Now's the time for the favor you owe me. You'll never be able to say that you didn't earn your success working for me," he said placing his thumb and forefinger on my chin so he could look into my eyes. My brain was trying to process what my body was feeling and at the same time trying to figure out what Carl was alluding to. As soon as I felt as though I was on the verge of saying something that made sense it no longer made sense to say it.

The only thing I did was nod my head as Carl got up with my hand in his and helped me up. Still barefoot I enjoyed the soft carpet between my toes, massaging my feet. It seemed as though all my senses were heightened, or were they? I had no idea what I was feeling or what I thought was going on. All I knew is that wonderful things were going on inside me.

The next thing I knew the door the man walked through was getting closer, then Carl gently whispered, "Remember our deal, I help you, you help me. You're on your way. You do whatever he says and if he tells me that you were as good a girl as I think you can be, you'll have the solo career you dream about. It'll be better than you could ever imagine." We stopped at the door and Carl knocked twice. The door opened slowly as Carl walked me just inside the room, then backed away quietly pulling it closed as he left. The man came toward me and reached behind my neck to unzip my dress as I stood there stoned in the name of my dream.

CHAPTER 17

Diane

Reality sets in

"*Where am I?*" I asked myself quietly as I sat up leaning back on my elbows. I closed my eyes trying to push the grogginess away and moved my legs back and forth like scissors enjoying the smooth softness of the expensive sheets. Looking around the room I tried to locate something familiar about it, but there was nothing. Sitting up further against the headboard I shivered against the cold I felt on my bare back. I looked down and realized that I was completely naked. A wave of shock shot through me as my mind scrambled to understand what events lead me to the king sized room I obviously spent the night in.

I looked toward the door and saw my dress on the floor a few steps in front of it. I got up wrapping the sheet around me like a toga then dropped it when I saw a fluffy white robe lying across a chaise that was beneath a window halfway between the bed and the door. I didn't see my shoes then looked down at my feet wiggling my toes. My memory was jarred a little after that. I remembered the slow, floaty walk to a door.

I opened the door and saw the colorful fabric hanging carefree but the excitement of the night before was no longer there. Only the trash left behind by those in attendance stood out.

"Diane."

I heard my name called and spun around. The voice came from behind me but I remembered being alone in the room.

"Diane," the voice said again.

"Yes?" I answered not knowing whether I was really hearing the voice or imagining it.

"Freshen up and meet me in the main hall as soon as you can."

"*Carl?*" I asked myself. Then it all came together. The slow walk to the room, the pill, the couple, the man, the door, and... "Oh my goodness! No, no, no, noooo," I said over and over again then I slapped a hand over my mouth then the other. "Oh my goodness!" I screamed into my hands shutting the bedroom door behind me and looking up to the ceiling at the loud speaker. I locked the door then headed to the bathroom.

About fifteen minutes later I began my walk through my Arabian nightmare barefoot wearing the dress I dreaded. As I approached the table I sat at the night before I stopped and stooped down to see if I could reach my shoes. Unfortunately there were no shoes beneath the table. Continuing on and wondering what I was going to wear on my feet I opened the door to exit the room and entered the main hallway.

"This way Ms. Frazier," a woman said appearing out of nowhere. "Carl is waiting for you out back." She led me down a long hall that was more like a corridor. There were several doors on each side of the hall that had nameplates on them. I believe the nameplates were a description of the theme of each room such as "The Beach". I imagined beach chairs, sand for a floor, a pool of water somehow looking like a little piece of the Pacific, and maybe a boardwalk. Being as rich as Carl anything could be done. I hoped to be as rich as or richer than Carl one day.

"Ah Diane," Carl said standing up to greet me. The woman nodded at Carl and he returned the nod releasing her from his presence. "You'll find your shoes, purse, and overnight bag on the chair behind you," he said sitting down beneath the shade of a palm tree that was somehow growing through an area of the porch. It was beautiful back there. Beyond Carl lay the Pacific Ocean in all its splendor. It was free to rush upon the shore and fall back swinging as it pleased. It was breathtaking.

"Diane," Carl said getting down to business. "Thank you for helping me out last night. My most distinguished guest was most pleased. When my guests are pleased I'm pleased," he said closely examining his buffed and polished nails. "As you'll come to know while working for me such favors will be required of you from time to time. These are special favors that I require that prove to me that you really want what you came to me to get. You want a successful solo singing career, I can make it happen. I can do anything because anything requires money and I have lots of it, more of it than most. Do you understand?"

"Yes sir," I answered not knowing whether to continue calling him Carl or not.

"Let me show you something," he said pulling what looked like a letter-sized post card from a folder inside his briefcase. I could see that it had my name on it. "This is you. This is how I see you," he said pointing to some handwritten information and numbers. It was some kind of report card. It had my name at the top, and my current and soon to be address as well. I immediately clammed up because no one knew about my new place. That was my place. He showed me my bank account information and everything that meant something to my life in California. In my heart I knew he could dig deeper if he wanted to and trace my life back to New Jersey.

I looked at Carl with "why?" on my face once again and he answered saying, "Because I need to know I can trust my girls," he said patting my hand, the hand that was thumbing through my new life in his folder.

"See, here is last night, and here is what you need to get in order to reach the next level. I have something special planned for you very soon that will enable you to work your way up to the next level. I'm doing this because I like you Diane. I don't like all my girls. But I like you. Now, any questions?"

"Yes, I don't know how to ask this any other way but why did last night have to happen Carl? What does last night have to do with me signing a contract to sing under your label?" I asked surprised at my guts.

"I see you didn't listen to what I said because if you had you'd know it has everything to do with it. Once you signed your name on the dotted line you became the property of me. You will do as I say and live your wildest dreams under my control or you'll walk, never speaking a word to anyone and ending up with less than what you had when I first met you. If you think you'll open your mouth you better think real hard before you do. I have ways of making you wish you never set foot in California." He reached into the briefcase again and pulled out a video tape.

"This is a little added incentive for you to keep moving in the right direction. It's a recording of your night with my distinguished guest. If you get out of hand this will get out of my hands and into the hands of some people that can make this one of your worst nightmares, and this is only the beginning," he said staring me down then cutting his eyes away from me like he tends to do when he's finished speaking to you.

"Oh, here's a little something for being a good girl,' he said pulling a white envelope from the briefcase. That's $2,000, which serves as a bonus. A car is waiting for you out front. I see your schedule will be quite busy for the next several months. I may call on you again sometime soon though. Oh, and congratulations on your new place. It makes me feel good knowing that I'm responsible for helping you earn the money to purchase it," he said smiling a smile I wanted to erase with the heel of one of my shoes. Realizing I was dismissed I stood up to leave but before turning around Carl motioned for me to come to him, which I did obediently. He stood up and opened his arms that offered false security and kissed me on my cheek then sent me on my way like the good little girl he knew I'd be because I had nothing and no one else to help me make my dreams comes true.

CHAPTER 18

Diane

My big mistake

The next day was Sunday and as I woke up Carla was walking in singing to herself and carrying several large shopping bags.

"Where on earth have you been?" I asked angrily as I threw back the covers and followed her to her closet.

"Hello to you too," she said pulling clothes from the bags and putting them away in various places.

"Listen, we have to talk now! I am so mad right now Carla I could rip your face off!" I shouted.

"Hey, knock it off in there," one of the girls yelled out from across the hall.

Carla whipped her head around quick as a flash and pointed her finger in my face saying, "First of all you better be grateful to me girl! All you've done is complain! So what, you gave it up, big deal! You probably don't even remember doing it! Get over it! I did and I do, she said shoving an expensive looking box of perfume in my face so I could see the price tag.

"Carla, I'm not like that," I said for some reason trying to convince her.

"Oh, but you are that type of girl Diane. There are a lot of girls like us and there's nothing to be ashamed of." Carla's attitude was getting to be too much for me but I somehow calmed down a bit.

"So that's what you were doing when I got back from touring? I saw the date and the address on the nightstand."

"Yup, and I'm flying out to New York for a while to shoot scenes for my movie."

"Carla you lied to me," I said defeated, following her around the room as she continued to put away the things she'd just bought. I followed her around as if she would turn around and say, "Surprise! I was just fooling around. All this isn't really happening!" But I knew that would never happen.

"Carla he recorded everything. I don't know how he did it nor can I prove anything but I don't think he'd lie."

"No, he's not lying," she said matter of factly. "Oh girl relax Tina has been working for Carl for several years now and so has Allison. He just uses it to scare you. He records me every time too," she said not caring.

"Carla this isn't what I wanted. I –"

"Oh, so you want to be back at Marlene House working at that filthy diner and checking the newspaper for jobs or waiting for the next little contest to be held? Sweetheart, in this world you have to know someone to make it in this game, and I'll tell you something else, I'm not going down with you if you turn into Tina number two because I've already fallen from grace once. I learned my lesson and you better learn too!" she spat out brushing past me and leaving me in the room.

"What am I gonna do? What am I gonna do?"

After confronting Carla I got busy getting my things together. Gregory my agent left a few messages about the purchase being a smooth and quick process because the owners were in a hurry to sell and move overseas. He said I should be living in the new place no later than midweek.

So much for friends. Carla truly disappointed me and now I had no one. I was prepared to never talk to her again but then I had second thoughts about it and decided that I may need to keep some form of communication going between us because I didn't want to be on her bad side.

I remembered Carla working with Sanya and Allison to keep Tina and I from talking. I absolutely couldn't trust Carla. Here I thought I was moving in with a friend and she turned on me. I was determined to talk with Tina alone outside the house to find out what she'd been trying to tell me. After getting more of my things together I showered and dressed thinking of a plan to let Tina know I needed to talk to her.

I decided on a simple plan. I'd write a quick note like "Need to talk. Meet me at so and so in fifteen minutes." I'd write it on a small piece of paper and ball it up like trash. I figured we'd make eye contact then I'd get her to see the ball without anyone around noticing then carefully drop it on the floor and keep walking like noting happened.

I was actually a little nervous because I didn't' know just how deep everyone's loyalty was to Carl. I wrote the note real quick, balled it up, then grabbed the trashcan from the upstairs bathroom as a prop. Tina wasn't in the hallway, she didn't meet me on the stairs, and she wasn't in the kitchen by herself. The girl was in the den sitting between Sanya and Allison watching a Reverend Ike type program! Things couldn't have been harder for me.

I didn't know what to do then. If I was living in a house with regular people I could just walk in there and tell Tina I needed to talk to her, but because I didn't want she nor I to get into any kind of trouble I had to be sneaky about it.

I'd just seen Carla leave the house so I didn't have to worry about her. Standing there in the hall with my back against the wall I held my note in one hand and the trashcan in the other. I had no creative idea and was about to go back upstairs when the phone rang. "I got it," I said as I darted across the hall to the kitchen. I picked it up and no one was there. The busy tone sounded, but I kept talking. "Uh, yes, she is. Hold on please," I said grinning. "Tina!" I yelled from the kitchen, "Phone call for you!" I quickly laid the phone down and ran upstairs to the end of the hall to the top of the steps that lead to the office. I saw Tina pick up the phone and aimed at her head.

"Hello? Hello? Hey!" she said turning around seeing me at the top of the stairs. I pointed frantically at the paper ball I'd just popped her in the head with. I mouthed "read it" and opened my hands and moved my head left to right like I was reading something. She bent down, picked it up, and uncrumpled it. She read the note, gave me a thumbs up, balled the note up again, and put it in her pocket.

"Uh-huh. Uh huh, okay yes. Okay bye," Tina faked then hung up. I pointed to the sliding doors in the dining room, pointed to myself then walked my fingers in the air indicating I wanted to slip out that way. She nodded, walked into the dining room to make sure no one was looking then waved for me to hurry.

I tiptoed down the stairs, into the dining room, and out the door. Once outside I peaked around the building looking for Carla's car. When I didn't see it I darted across the street and ran between two apartment buildings to get to the next block. I didn't take the streets because I didn't want to chance Carla seeing me.

A few blocks and several minutes later I reached the car wash I told Tina to meet me at and waited. Finally, she pulled up and I hopped in the car with her. "Good idea," she said rolling up her window as the car slowly pulled into the wash.

"So what's going on?" I asked.

"Girlfriend," Tina began, "you're into something that you know nothing about." She looked me up and down as if we hadn't been living in the same house for over a year. "You're not even built for this, you don't even have what it takes," she said after a while. "Carla doesn't care about you. All you are to Carla is a stepping stone. She used you to get what she's been wanting."

"What do you mean?" I asked.

"What I mean is that Carla is a sort of recruit for Carl's little racket he's got going. She's been living here for years but when Carl wants a new girl he sends girls like Carla out to pick up new talent so to speak." By this time the car had gone through the wash and was being dried by the attendants. Before the front of the car was completely out I ducked and laid the seat back as far as it would go and we continued talking with me unseen by anyone driving or walking by. We finally pulled out onto the street and continued talking.

"So you mean to tell me that all along she was playing a role? So she never lived at the boarding house?" I asked hurt because I once considered Carla a friend. Hurt because I was so easily fooled.

"Oh no, she really used to live there before getting hooked up with Carl."

"Do you know how she met him?"

"From what I heard he picked her up at a disco she was working at and she's been working for him ever since."

Lying there looking at the sky through the windshield as Tina drove I thought. I thought about whether there were any holes in anything Carla ever said to me. I wondered if I'd paid a little more attention to our encounters would I be in the same situation I was in at that moment. Then as if Marlene was right there, I heard her voice clear as day. I remembered our conversation on my rented bed in her home. She told me that Carla was a prostitute and that the Hispanic girl that showed up at Marlene's house one night was someone Carla had influenced. I described the girl to Tina and she knew right away who she was.

"That's Consuela," she said. "She used to model just like me. Sometimes we'd go out together. She was nice."

"Well, what happened to her?"

Shaking her head and briefly closing and opening her eyes she said, "Consuela's out walking the block these days."

"What do you mean?"

"I mean she's out on the street corners for Carl."

"What?"

"Yes, Carl has girls on every level. Some start at the bottom and remain there, while others work their way up," then a brief pause and she continued, "Like me," she revealed. "Are you surprised?"

"Of course I am!" I said.

"See, because you have real talent Carl is able to get the most out of you. He makes money from your talent on stage and ... you know the rest."

We were on the highway in the slow lane headed for nowhere, and I realized for the first time my singing career was headed in the same direction.

"Earlier you said that Carla used me as a stepping stone. How is that," I asked.

"Well Carla started out on the block just like me then she was given the opportunity to make more money and move up. When Carl explained what favors she had to return in order to get there she got busy. It was her idea to live a fake life at the boarding house because she'd lived there long enough to know the types of people that end up living there," she said changing lanes.

"And there I was with my eyes big with the hope of being some famous singer and I ended up getting fooled," I said, my emotions even more tender. "Carla once told me about meeting some director guy that wanted her to have sex with him in order to get a role but she turned him down. She said he made getting work in L.A. hard for her because he told everyone not to hire her. Was that true?" I asked hoping everything Carla told me wasn't true.

"That's partially true," Tina said. "The only thing is that there was no director. She was talking about Carl. When she met Carl and he told her he could make her a star he laid everything on the table telling her what he expected from her. She refused and left. But when your stomach is empty and the nights are cold you start thinking that compromising your morals isn't such a bad thing."

"So she lied to me about that too. I'm such a fool."

"Diane, don't beat yourself up about it because if I was in your shoes I probably would've done the same thing. A lot of girls would've." I thought about Consuela, wondering why she fell from grace so I asked.

Tina responded saying, "One day she and Carl got into an argument over a party he wanted her to attend. She told him that she couldn't

143

because her mother had fallen ill and she needed to visit her. He told her that she was his property and that she'd better be at the party. Well, that night Consuela bought a plane ticket and flew out to Texas, not caring about Carl and his rule. She'd only been there a few hours before opening the door and being snatched up by some of Carl's men. They flew back here and she's been demoted to the block ever since. That was three or four years ago I think."

After hearing Consuela's story I got scared. Thoughts of leaving my career behind had crossed my mind several times since my talk with Carl, but I wasn't so sure that it would be easy. "What did you do not to be able to work for a few months?" I asked.

"Allison overheard me on the telephone talking to my sister about how much I hate Carl because of how he treats us and she told. The next thing I knew Carl sent a car to take me to his home in Brentwood and he threatened me and hit me then to ld me I couldn't work for a while," she said with trembling lips.

"I'm so sorry," I said wanting to hug her but not wanting to risk being seen.

"Thanks, but its okay – really. I need the money to make a living and to send to my family in China. When I think of them what I do isn't so bad because my family is my motivation."

"Is there anything I can do to get out of the contract with Carl?"

"Yeah."

"What is it?"

"Die."

Stunned, I sank deeper into the seat and tears welled up in my eyes. The excitement of my career and the excitement of moving into my own place vanished, just like that.

"And you wanna know something else?"

"No, not really."

"Carla isn't even her real name."

"It isn't?!" I asked surprised and sat up.

"No, it isn't, and lay back down," she scolded. "Her real name is Heather Daniels. Probably everything she's told you is a lie. I'm sorry," she said.

"No, it's alright. It's my fault anyway. I was being impatient and wanted everything right away. Do you ever pray Tina?"

"Yeah, I do sometimes," she said. "Like before bed and in the morning and when I need help."

"I never really pray," I said playing with my fingers. "Tina I don't know what to do."

"And I don't know what to tell you to do," she said softly and patted me on the thigh. "Well, that's it. That's all I know honey. You deserve to know that. Look at it this way, you got involved with Carla and Carl because you didn't know what you were doing, didn't read the fine print." She continued driving. "Oops, there's one more thing I forgot to mention. It has to do with the contract."

"What on earth else is there?"

"You're not gonna like this, but like I said you deserve to know and it's better that you're hearing from me than from a liar like Carla or not knowing at all."

"What is it?"

"Well, there's a part of the contract that was in small print that can affect you forever. My heart beat irregularly as I waited. "The contract states that Carl has the right to fifty percent of all the taxable earnings you make no matter what it is. If you decide to sell cars he gets fifty percent, if you want to be a housekeeper, fifty percent, if you want to run a daycare out of your home, fifty percent. He called himself being lenient with this part because instead of saying he wanted half of your income for the rest of your life, he decided that thirty years was enough. I'm sorry."

"What am I gonna do?"

"Well, the first thing you need to do is get back home before I burn all my gas. I shouldn't complain so much though because gas prices aren't as high as they were several months ago. Thank God that's over," she said heading in the direction of home. Several blocks from home I told Tina to drop me off and I'd walk the rest of the way.

Walking, I thought about my life and how I came to California on my own. I thought about the competition I'd won second place in. Classique. Carla. Carl. Marlene. Mom and dad. Sharon and everyone and everything. Now, after almost two years it was all about to blow up in my face, just go up in smoke.

I didn't know where to go, where to turn. I had no friends. Carla was a lie. Tina was just someone who had pity for me and my dumb self. She was right though, she read the contract and accepted its terms. However, me in my impatience signed my name on the line in ignorance. At that moment I felt like the biggest failure, the biggest fool. A huge heaviness blanketed me again but instead of wanting to throw it off I easily welcomed it because I was used to the depression the heaviness brought with it.

I made all the wrong decisions and one after another they leaped upon me in a heap and weighed on me. I desperately wanted to talk to Sharon but I knew she'd detect something wrong in my voice. No, I couldn't call her because I didn't want to reveal my failure in a moment of weakness. Sometimes my sister had the ability to get information out of me, but not this time. I was not going to call her. Officially alone I accepted the voluntary solitude and continued walking up the walkway, through the door, and to my room.

After my talk with Tina I felt like the biggest clown. I was an idiot. Carla was in the room and watched me as I busied myself with gathering bags and boxes. I decided not to take anything with me that I didn't bring when I came or purchased since I moved in. That meant the bed that Carla ordered and had delivered to the house for me was staying as well as the friendship charm and necklace that Carla gave me. I snatched it from my neck and dropped it on my bed. I made several trips back and forth to my car until I had one bag left that I planned to lay across my lap as I drove.

Noticing that I picked up my last bag Carla spoke up saying, "I would've helped out but the way you kept glaring at me scared me away," she said trying to evoke an emotional moment. She had no idea of how through with her I was and she was trying to have a sentimental moment because I was moving out. I so wanted to grab her by the face and slam her head into the wall but I kept my cool. I allowed her cover to remain in tact. She stood up and walked toward me with her arms outstretched for a hug and I reluctantly accepted her embrace.

Am I in the Twilight Zone? I silently asked myself. *Does Carla really expect me to be okay with being signed to a label that runs a prostitution ring and threatens to take any wages I make if I leave?* Releasing Carla from a forced embraced I silently turned and left.

CHAPTER 19

Diane

Some pleasure in pain

I booked a room at a nice hotel not too far from my condo. I couldn't bear staying another night under the same roof as Carla, Allison, and Sanya. I imagined them curled up around Carl's feet looking up to him as their master. Carla was on his lap being petted as she purred because she's teacher's pet. I shook the image from my mind as I carried a few bags into the hotel, then I thought about dinner. I didn't know whether to order take out, room service, or go to a restaurant. After a few moments I decided to go out, get some fresh air, relax, and be waited on after all I'd been through and discovered.

I called the front desk and asked for restaurant suggestions. The clerk told me about an establishment called Seth's. I'd heard about it before but never got the chance to check it out. Seth's is an upscale restaurant that a lot of celebrities and people that want to be seen frequent. I couldn't wait to go.

Before I reached the door all the delicious smells wafted into the evening air calling me inside. The doors were opened for me and I was taken to a table immediately. Even though I'm not a mega star people still recognize me when I go out. I must admit I love the attention that being a star brings.

After ordering my drink and appetizer I relaxed in my chair and scanned the room. I saw quite a few celebrities there and I almost freaked out but quickly calmed when I reminded myself of who *I* was. I watched as people almost broke their necks to see what the celebrities were wearing and eating and who they were dining with. Deep down inside I was jealous. I was jealous that I was sitting there, a celebrity in my own right, and no one was gawking at me. All I got were glances and little whispers every now and then but that's it.

While sampling my appetizer, I noticed a low murmur all around me. I looked up and people were whispering to each other and looking toward the door. I didn't want to seem like I was interested in seeing who'd just come in but my curiosity got the best of me.

Turning around slowly while fluffing my hair with my hand to make people think I could really care less, I caught a glimpse of one of the most beautiful men I've ever seen. *"Who is he?"* I whispered to myself, then I caught myself and looked around real quick hoping no one noticed that I was as enchanted by this man as they were.

He was impeccably dressed in a suit that was obviously made just for him. His skin was the smoothest, deepest brown I'd ever seen and his eyes, his eyes… Well, that did it for me. *"He's a fox,"* I said under my breath as the owner of Seth's led the man to what looked to be the best table in the restaurant. I was so grateful that from where I sat I could see him clearly without making a great effort to. I deliberately began chewing my food slower, then I picked up my glass and took sips of my juice to prolong my stay there.

I was sweating. I'd never reacted to a guy like that before. I wondered what was wrong with me. The door opened again and a gorgeous woman walked in alone and I secretly hoped she wasn't headed to the same table as my future husband I was contemplating on stalking. Thankfully, she was led to another part of the restaurant but not without getting eyed by almost every man and a few women in the building.

So he remained alone at his table. Feeling brave I broke away from my partial vigil of him to finish my meal before it got cold. I noticed that there were only two other people dining alone that evening besides my guy and I. One was a woman who seemed to be engrossed with paperwork and the other a man who kept checking his watch. All of a sudden I felt it was a bad idea to dine alone because I didn't know what to do with myself.

Although you're there to eat something's missing if there's no conversation. I began to feel lonely and awkward and wondered if people noticed. I shifted in my seat and my fork fell from my plate to the floor. Immediately my waiter was on his way with another. Just before ordering my dessert a different waiter pardoned himself and said that I'd been invited to have my dessert at Mr. Anderson's table.

He moved from my field of vision and did an elegant sweeping motion with his arm gesturing toward my guy's table. "Are you sure?" I asked.

"Yes madam, I am quite sure. This way please," he said after pulling my chair out and helping me up. I grabbed my purse and walked to my guy's table with more confidence than I actually felt. He stood before I reached the table and pulled my chair out for me.

"Thank you Hermon," he said smoothly. Please return in a few minutes to take our dessert requests." After he was seated we both spoke at the same time and I nervously pulled away from his gaze to pick up a flute of water. I wanted to gulp down the whole glass to refresh my suddenly dry mouth but I was in the presence of too much beauty to do something so unrefined.

"I'm sorry, you speak first," he said with a voice that I can only describe as silky bass.

"Thank you for inviting me to your table," I managed to say.

"And thank you for accepting my invitation," he responded. I had it bad and I had not known what "it" was until that day. There was something chemical going on between us, at least with me. My heart was beating fast and I was sweating in places I didn't think people sweated, like above my top lip and beneath my lower one. I was an overall mess. I prayed my natural hair hadn't started drawing up as I felt a trickle of sweat slide down my back bone. I wanted to run to the bathroom to get myself under control but it was too late.

"I noticed you immediately once I sat down. I thought you were waiting for someone. If I'd known you were dining alone I would've invited you over sooner," he said then he smiled. He smiled a glowing, straight smile. He was perfect and smelled like the best part of all delicious scents whose essence was perfected, bottled, and worn by only him. He amazed me. I looked around for a moment and noticed all the eyes that were watching us. "Don't mind them, but I'm sure you're used to it."

"I'm getting used to it," I said trying to act modest.

"Don't worry, you will. You'll have to with all the fans you have. Classique makes some great music. I have all your albums and I play them everyday. My favorite on your first album is *It's Me* and my new favorite is *Invite Me In*.

"I sing lead on both of them," I blushed.

"I know."

Just in time the waiter returned for our dessert orders.

"What would you like madam?"

"I think the apple pie and walnut ice cream sounds good."

"I'll have the same."

As we waited for the waiter to return we talked. "You know," I began, "you look very familiar. I can't remember where I've seen you, but I know I've seen you somewhere. What do you do?"

"Oh, I'm a businessman. I'm in the trucking industry."

"I know where I've seen you. You've been in the newspaper, magazines, and you've been on talk shows because you're a business genius." I could tell he was as flattered by me as I was by him.

"I wouldn't say a genius. I'm far from it." I only smiled because I knew better.

"So, how did you end up in L.A.?" I asked more comfortable with him.

"Hey, that was my next question for you."

"Okay," I said, "I'll go first. Well, as you already know I sing. Um, I wasn't getting anywhere pursuing my career in Jersey, so when I heard there was going to be a singing contest in L.A. I packed up and headed here to enter the contest hoping to win. I told my story to a magazine once. I thought anyone who wanted to know knew that."

"I did, but I wanted to hear it from you. So, how did you end up with Berdynu Records?"

"Actually, I met a girl and we became friends then she set up a meeting for me with the president of Berdynu Records and the rest is history," I explained forcing a smile at the sour memory.

"Interesting. Sounds like you have someone very special in your corner."

"Yeah, I guess so. Now your turn," I said glad to turn the spotlight away from myself for once. "How did you end up in L.A.?"

"Well, I felt it was time to leave home. My mom and sister had everything they needed so I felt secure leaving to start the next chapter of my life. I met a man who had a company, he hired me, he promoted me, I learned about the business from the bottom up from the best, and the next thing I know I helped create an empire."

"Wow, sounds like *you* were the one with someone special in your corner," I said nudging his hand playfully with mine, and then spoke again asking, "Have you gone back to visit?"

"No, my schedule really doesn't allow me that kind of free time, but soon I'm going to make the time to visit my mom and sister."

"I haven't gone back either. Actually, I was in New York for a concert a while back and my family came to see me. That's the closest *I've* come to visiting home."

"You sound like you really don't want to go back."

"Hmm, maybe I don't," I said looking away briefly.

"I'm not gonna touch that subject because it takes the smile from your face," he said bringing my smile back. Our desserts came a few moments later and we enjoyed the decadent tastes and continued chatting about this and that, then his face became serious as he spoke again.

"Diane, I've enjoyed meeting you and I know you have a hectic schedule as well as I, but I'd like to see you again if you'd agree to it."

Careful not to answer too eagerly I finished chewing, swallowed, and then said, "Of course, I'd love to see you again." Embarrassed that "love" escaped from my heart and out of my mouth I shoved another spoonful in to keep myself quiet.

"I'd like to call you. May I have your number?" The question in his voice, and the way he asked it let me know that he actually believed there was a chance I'd say no. Gladly, I reached inside my purse for a pen and something to write on, but he was quicker and pulled out two business cards. He handed me one and I wrote my number down. I slid it to him and he gave me the other card telling me I could call him anytime and what to do if he couldn't take my call for whatever reason.

"You know you're not the first person I've met in L.A. that's from Jersey."

"Oh really? I haven't met anyone from Jersey let alone South Jersey. No one's ever heard of Blue Anchor or Chesilhurst. They look at you like you're from some backwoods town where you have to walk a mile to get anywhere." James gave me a "come on now" type of look. We both laughed because the nearest bus stop or the nearest anything was at least a mile from Chesilhurst.

"Stop it!" I said throwing a soft punch at his arm. "Don't talk about where I'm from. It's bad enough that I was bored to death growing up there. I was embarrassed to tell people that I lived there. That's why I claim Englewood most of the time when someone asks. It's a complete lie because I was only born there, not raised, but a lot of my family from both sides live there."

"You don't have to give me an explanation," he said leaning back in his chair grinning at me. Just then our waiter returned to the table with the bill. "I'll take care of the lady's dinner as well," he said handing the little folder back to the waiter with his credit card tucked inside. "How did you get here? Can I take you home?" he asked.

"Actually I drove myself," I said disappointed.

"I want to spend more time with you because I know I may not be able to see you for a least a month."

"Yes, I'm going to be quite busy," I said confirming the truth about my life. We looked at each other, then James stood and helped me from my seat. We walked through the restaurant briskly escaping laser beam stares and into the warm L.A. night. We slowly walked to my car utilizing every moment we could to spend time with each other before departing. We were silent almost the whole walk to the car then James spoke up a few yards before we reached it.

"Ever since I heard about you I wanted to meet you. I knew I would eventually because of connections but meeting you this way was better. I met you, now I want to know you. I can't explain why I feel like this or even why I'm saying these things to you when I just met you." He looked up for a moment taking a deep breath then looked at me again. "I've got to see you again – soon. Talking to you on the phone isn't going to be enough. Man, where is this coming from?" he asked himself out loud.

"I feel the same way," I said looking up at him. He opened my car door and I got in and rolled the window down not ready to be apart from him. He bent down and leaned in the window, and I closed my eyes waiting for his lips to touch mine but they never did. He lingered on my forehead and I was utterly embarrassed.

"I put it there so you'd think about me because I'm definitely going to be thinking about you. Be careful and call me when you get to your room."

"I will," I said thinking his line was a little corny and drove off with my heart glowing. Heat flushed through me and I stretched myself across the passenger seat to roll the window down thinking of the unexpected encounter I had at Seth's.

When I got to my room I jumped on the bed and called James. He was glad I called and we talked for about an hour then he made me promise to call him as soon as my new line was working so I could give him the number.

Later that night, close to midnight the phone rang. It was one of Carl's assistants. She said Carl wanted me to report to his Brentwood home the next evening for an engagement he was having, and not to worry about my attire. Hanging up, the heaviness returned. I was depressed because the success of my singing career hinged not just on my talent, album sales, and image but secretly being a whore.

I was living a lie. I lay across the bed thinking there was no place I could go and not be found by Carl's people. I felt helpless, afraid, and lost. I thought about Consuela for a moment. She thought she was going to get on a plane and visit her sick mother in Texas. What made me think that I could check into a hotel in L.A. and not be tracked down?

I was ashamed of myself for not being the woman I wanted to be. The woman I wanted to be would have told Carl off and not flinch at the mention of a blackmail video or financial attachments for thirty years. Instead I made up in my mind that I would obediently play by Carl's rules to save myself the embarrassment of failure and protect my treasured pride.

✃

The next day was Monday and I decided to call Gregory to find out about my condo.

"Good news, you can move in a day early. Do you need me to call a moving company for you?"

"Oh no, all I have are a few boxes and suitcases. I can handle them."

"Alright, why don't you swing by the office to sign a few more documents and pick up your keys, or if you'd like I can meet you at the building."

"I'd really appreciate it if you met me because I have an awful lot to do today and going to your part of the city would cost me too much time," I said glad that he gave me an option.

"Sure thing. I'll meet you there in an hour."

I quickly gathered my things, took a quick shower, checked out and was out the door headed for my new home. "Thank you," I said out loud. That was my attempt at thanking the God I wasn't sure existed unless I wanted or needed Him to. I drove on.

About fifteen minutes later I pulled into the lot and saw Gregory's car. He got out when he saw me pulling in. He was smiling and was still handsome, only he wasn't *as* handsome because of the things he said to me that still echoed in my mind every now and then.

"Diane! How are you?" He asked grinning and holding his arms out for a hug. "I know this isn't very professional but I can sense that you need a hug."

My smile went away as he wrapped me in his strong embrace. The bit of attraction I felt toward him melted away and was replaced with that of a daughter's affection for her father. I tensed as I felt myself surrendering to the pure love that emanated from this man named Gregory.

153

"Mmm, that was good," he said caressing my back in an "it's going to be alright" manner. The longer I was in Gregory's presence the stranger I felt because it was like he knew more, even more than what he'd said to me the week before. "There's a parking garage here as well, for a fee of course. I suggest you take advantage of it because people will notice that you live alone and they may want to take advantage of your vulnerability. Security is tight in this building but it's better to be safe than sorry."

"You're right. I'll be sure to do that."

"I'm not going to come in because I know you're pressed for time, so if you sign here and here we're done." I signed where he indicated and smiled.

"Here are your keys, the documents you need, and that's it. It's been a pleasure working with you." I could've let the conversation end like that but I felt I had to apologize for the way I reacted to the things he said to me the first time we met.

"Gregory, I'm sorry. I…"

"You don't have to apologize sweetheart. I was once where you are, just different circumstances. Don't worry about it." He patted me on the shoulder and we started off in opposite directions. "Diane," I heard behind me, and then I turned around. "No matter what situation you're in He," he said pointing upward, "can get you out." I nodded then he turned and continued walking.

I stood there a moment and filed that bit of information away with the other things he'd told me. In my mind they sat in a drawer with no label on it. I didn't know where they belonged.

CHAPTER 20

Diane

Double life

The first few hours of the day I moved my things in. I had so few possessions that the place still looked empty. There were some items at Marlene House that I'd wanted to pick up for a while but I was either too busy or leery about encountering Marlene. I didn't know what she'd have to say. I wondered what it would be like to see her again. Deep down inside I dreaded it, but there was also a part of me that wanted to confide in her for some reason.

I guess it was because she already knew what took me so long to realize about Carla. I didn't want Marlene to throw her accuracy about Carla in my face, but this time I won the battle against my pride and decided to visit Marlene House anyway.

During the drive over I rehearsed what I'd say. I had something planned for all the possible reactions I felt Marlene could have when seeing me. *"Diane relax,"* I told myself repeatedly. The last time I said it was just as I was about to put my hand on the doorknob. I took a deep breath and opened the door. I purposefully stopped by at a time I knew hardly anyone would be there. It was around two o'clock, so that meant lunch had already been served and eaten. The kitchen was spotless yet the scents created during the preparation and eating of the food still lingered in the air speaking to my flippity flopping stomach. I was nervous to see Marlene because truth was there before I left and that same truth remained.

I walked up to my old room and tried the knob. It was locked. I tried Carla's door and it too was locked. I turned to head back downstairs then heard loud laughter and talking then the screen door slam shut. It was Marlene. My heart tried to run a marathon in my chest and I put a hand on it and swallowed a big gulp or air. I slowly headed down the stairs to act like everything in my life was in order and I didn't need a shoulder to cry on.

"Well, look who decided to come back for her things, because I know you didn't come to visit me," Marlene said with a sly look. My stomach churned. "So how've you been?" she asked.

"Good, really good," I lied.

"I saw you on a billboard and on Soul Train. You have a beautiful voice honey. Okay now, I know you didn't come here to see me so let me go get my keys and I'll meet you in the basement," she said moving around me.

"Okay."

When she met me in the basement she flipped through the keys on a keychain until she found what she was looking for. She unlocked a big trunk that when opened had my clothes and shoes and well, everything I left behind in it. I noticed she had several other trunks like it.

"Here you go," she said in a sing songy voice. I grabbed the things I needed and left the remaining items.

"Do you still donate to Goodwill and the Salvation Army?" I asked.

"I sure do. Thanks."

Upstairs Marlene shut the door and we stood there for what I thought was an awkward eternity. "Okay then, thanks for everything," I said and headed for the door.

"Wait," Marlene said. "I'm not going to ask you where you've been or what your life is like now, but I know how life can be. "Here" she said swinging keys around then pulled off two of them. "I want you to hold on to these in case you need them. I know how life can be," she repeated. "I changed the locks to your room a few days after you didn't show up, but I decided not to rent the room out just in case you came back," she said with knowing eyes.

"But that's..." I began but Marlene cut me off.

"No-no. Don't you worry about it. I *want* to do this. I want the room vacant in case you need it. I had a room waiting for me and I want you to have one too." Trying to analyze what Marlene was relaying to me I almost became offended. I thought she was predicting failure in my life because hers failed. Then I remembered how relieved she said she was when she had nowhere else to go and Mrs. Petitti was there for her. Marlene wanted to be there for me in the same way.

"Thank you Marlene," I said, then found myself reaching out to hug her. I lingered there a little longer than expected almost softening to the point where I wanted to tell her everything, but I let go and left.

❦

I had to prepare for Carl's engagement, and his assistant said I didn't need to worry about what to wear. Although I'd only been to one of Carl's so-called engagements I felt it was odd that I didn't have to arrive there already dressed for whatever was going to happen. At the appropriate time a car arrived in front of my building. Settling down in the car I sat back with my eyes closed trying not to think about what lay ahead for me that evening. I felt small sitting there on the buttery soft leather seats. I felt like a child lost in the goings on of the adult world. Absolutely lost.

"Hello Ms. Frazier. Please follow me," an attractive middle-aged woman said. I followed her down a long hall that I didn't take the last time I was there. The woman stopped at a door almost at the very end of the hall. I could vaguely hear music pulsating on the other side. She nodded her head slightly in place of good bye and walked off.

I touched the doorknob and took a breath, then opened the door. It was some sort of dressing room. I felt like I was back in Vegas preparing for a concert with Classique. Girls were running around barely dressed and there were wigs, costumes, and high heels galore.

"You Diane?" Someone asked from behind me. I whipped around to see a short deep toned girl with big brown eyes staring up at me.

"Yeah," I said.

"I'm Kelly. Come with me."

We walked by at least twelve girls sitting at different stations doing their make up or having their make up done. "This is where you sit. You're next to me. I'm supposed to school you. You listen to me, get in get the job done, and you're out. None of us want to be here, but we've all got to be here for one reason or another." I stared at her. I wondered if she recognized me. She and I were about the same age and were probably into the same things like music. What was stopping her from recognizing me? What was stopping her from telling everyone that Diane from Classique is an undercover whore? I hesitated a bit as she tried to sit me down to begin working on my makeup.

"Listen honey, I don't know you. All I know is your name is Diane. Diane may not even be your real name. I really don't care. What I do know is that you're new to Level Two and it's my job to get you acquainted

157

with the rules. You must have done something right though because you're here. Every new level is a promotion."

"A promotion? A promotion for what?" I asked trying to find out what she knew.

"The higher you move up the closer you are to whatever it is you sought out Carl for in the first place. In my case I want to be an actress. Carl's gonna help me get my big break. I've had parts in soap operas and television series, but I want one of those parts that can make me Oscar worthy."

"I heard that," I said feigning interest.

"You know the people around here are big shots that come from all over the world. If we make them happy, they make Carl happy. Carl can make us happy. You know what I mean? Now this here thing is real simple. Carl provides us with the best makeup, costumes, and props. We can wear whatever we want. If there's something we want to wear or better yet if there's something one of Carl's guests requests we wear, all we have to do is let one of Carl's assistants know and it's done."

By that time Kelly had already put foundation, lipstick, eye shadow, eyeliner and an eyelash on me. Just as she was about to put the glue on my other lash I heard a familiar voice. It was Carla! I hadn't seen here since Sunday when I packed and left.

My eyes followed the voice until I laid eyes on her across the room at a vanity midway between the entrance in and the door that led to the party. My heart beat quicker and the knuckles on my hands began to ache. Nerves.

"Okay, you're all done. All you have to do is pick a wig. You know, although I hate this job, it's kind of fun getting dressed up everyday because you get to act like someone you're not. I love disguising myself. I just keep telling myself that it's another role and it helps every time."

I stood up and studied the wigs. Most were long but some were short bob styles and all were in every color imaginable. I chose an electric blue one that had a straight bang and the rest of the hair was straight and came down long to my waist.

"Ooh girl that wig looks dynamite on you! There's a teddy on the rack that will go perfectly with it. Here", she said, kicking off her silver heels, "Size eight right?" she asked pushing them toward me.

"Yeah," I said trying them on. "Thanks." Walking to the rack I glanced over at Carla sitting down like Queen Bee. She must've been telling an interesting story. About five or six girls gathered around her laughing when she laughed. I found the teddy and snatched it from the rack, hanger and all. Carla's makeup completed, she sashayed by the rack I was ducking behind. She took something from a tray a girl was guarding then grabbed a partial face mask from a shelf before entering the party.

I took note of her outfit before she stepped out so I could locate her once I entered the party myself. She was dressed as a flapper and if I didn't despise her I would've thought she looked cute. Making my way over to Kelly I looked around to see if I recognized anyone else. No one. I grabbed a sponge and got to work applying Kelly's foundation. Fifteen minutes later we were both ready to go.

"Here, take one," Kelly said.

"What's this?"

"It's something that makes what we do for a living bearable. It's not as strong as what Carl likes to have handed out but it still takes the edge off. Try one." I took one and swallowed it without hesitation. I decided I'd have to buy some of my own to get through my favors for Carl and to take at home to forget what I did.

Stepping inside the party I realized Carl's home was much larger than I thought. We were standing in a lounge within his home. It was complete with a stage, tables, and everything else you'd expect to see at a lounge, even a live band. If I wasn't forced to be there in the name of my career I probably would've enjoyed myself. Walking side by side Kelly and I took in everything.

"See over there," she said, "That's Ivy. She's been here the longest, but I don't' know why she hasn't been promoted because she good at what she does. As a matter of fact she's probably the best girl at this level. Watch her."

Ivy slithered across the room to a guy wearing glasses that had a nerdy look going on. She looped her arm through his and led him over to a couch. Satisfied that he wasn't going anywhere she skipped over to the bar to get him something to drink and she soon convinced him to finish the glass.

Bored watching Ivy I asked, "So how does this work?"

"Well, our job is to make sure none of Carl's guests are alone no matter what. If you see a girl has walked away for a moment you can pick up where she left off unless he specifically requests her. Sometimes they request more than one girl if you know what I mean." I cringed at her words. "Hey, you're a big girl now, making big girl decisions," she said looking serious.

Okay, it's my time, I see a lone wolf," she said straightening her wig and adjusting herself.

Standing alone near a tall plant my gaze fell on Ivy again. She'd managed to take the guy's glasses off and had them on her head. His tie and the neck of his buttoned shirt were undone. She'd played around with his hair so much that it stood on end and his face was covered with red lip prints.

"*She is good,*" I said to myself. "*This isn't me,*" I thought as the tiny pill Kelly gave me kicked in. "*I can't do this.*" With my back against the wall I noticed three men entering the room. All the ladies were occupied except for me and another girl. I saw everyone's eyes dart in their direction like they were well known or regulars.

Each of them was very well dressed in expensive suits, but their backs were turned to me so I couldn't see their faces. Adjusting my mask and then my outfit I walked slowly over to the three men going over what I'd say and which one I'd talk to. I wondered what he would say and want me to do. Just before I reached them, all three of them turned around to take in the rest of the lounge and I made a serious beeline toward a dim corner of the room!

"*Is that James?!*" I asked out loud through shortened breaths. I didn't know whether to be upset that he was there, embarrassed that I was there, or relieved that I had a mask on and he didn't recognize me. I pulled back further into the corner to keep an eye on him and watched two girls approach them who appeared to be familiar with his friends.

I was torn between going to him so no one else could spend time with him and keeping my distance so I wouldn't be recognized. I felt a little silly for thinking that after meeting once he'd be able to recognize me in disguise in such a setting. I took a step away from my hiding place then stopped in my tracks as my arch enemy swooped down on the man I wanted to be mine.

Smoldering with rage I clenched my fists wishing Carla's neck was in them. She grabbed his hand and led him over to a couch along a wall. Realizing I wasn't doing my job I scoped the room for a lonely man. Seeing one, I walked over to him and sat down at his table. He smiled at me and asked me my name. I gave him a random one. I think he picked up on it because he asked me if I was sure. I just smiled.

"What's yours?" I asked not caring.

"Love."

"Love, huh? That's different," I said still thinking about James.

Then all of a sudden Love looked at me then seemed to look inside me. Instantly I felt ashamed to be near him and moved to get up. He touched my hand gently and both my shame and my high left. I didn't imagine it. I felt something like a wave of electricity go through me and I somehow knew it would have a lasting impression on me. I looked away briefly to see if anyone noticed what was going on then feeling scatterbrained I asked him his name again but he was gone.

Afraid that I'd imagined him after all I sat like stone trying to rationalize what I was pretty sure was real. I looked around then placed my hand on the seat Love sat on. It was warm. "Okay that proves he was here but it doesn't explain where he is now." Shaking my head then standing up I walked the room looking for another guy. I saw one.

I walked up to him noticing I hadn't seen him all night. His head was bent toward a plate full of food so I couldn't get a good look at him. When I reached him I touched his arm and he raised his head. Those eyes! Those eyes! I don't know how but it was him again! He was a completely different man in different clothes! He was even a different race! But he had the same eyes that shined like diamonds and seemed like forever!

While my hand was still on his arm every hair on my body stood on end. I was drawn to him and wanted to cry. No it was much deeper than that. I wanted to weep. Thinking I wouldn't be able to stand on my wobbly legs much longer, I backed away from him and his awesome presence and stumbled into a guest. Composing myself I saw Kelly and ran over to her almost knocking her over.

"What's wrong with you?" she asked looking at me like I was crazy.

"Nothing. Nothing," I said as I fanned my face with my hands trying to cool the heat that rushed there. Regaining my composure I looked around and spotted James. Carla still had her talons in him and there was nothing I could do. By now every man was taken care of. Many left the lounge with a girl through one of several doors in the back of the room and I scanned the room frantically.

I turned to go to Love, thinking I could pair up with him but he'd vanished again, so I was left with no one.

There hadn't been any new men for the past hour or so, so I figured things were winding down. Satisfied, I made myself busy by offering to serve drinks. I walked around asking for orders and delivering them, all the while keeping my eyes on Carla and James. His eyes roamed the room while Carla tried to keep his attention. He turned his head one way then she turned it back. Every now and then he checked his watch then he took a quick peak around. I assumed he was looking for the two guys he came with.

I felt triumphant inside although Carla was sitting on his lap. I was triumphant because he didn't show much interest in Carla. I saw relief on his face when he turned once more because his two friends stumbled into the room through a door, looking disheveled. A moment later Ivy followed with no expression on her face whatsoever.

At that time James assisted Carla off his lap and stood up. He reached for his wallet and handed her some bills. His friends walked over to him and he was furious but kept his control when he spoke to them. Carla stood up counting the bills with a satisfied look on her face. She tucked them safely inside her bra and looked for the next man. I wondered whether James made a habit of paying women for their time.

I wanted to run to him asking why he was there but how foolish I'd be for doing that. I was living two lives and could never let James know about the mess I'd gotten myself into. The whole night I hadn't paid much attention to anything because I was in my own world and confused about James' presence there as well as my strange encounter at Carl's.

Stealing a peak at James and his friends again as they approached the exit a familiar song began playing. I felt eerie. It was Classique. It was *If You Only Knew* and I was singing lead. How sad that I was standing there half naked about twenty feet away from a guy I'd just met and that I wanted to get to know better, knowing full well he'd never know everything about me.

I remained in that spot listening to the me I loved, the me I was proud of, the me that was free from the prison of the me I hated and wanted to hide. Finally brave enough, I remained in that spot as James and the two guys walked by not noticing me, Diane from Classique, but his friends noticed me, the thing that was there for their pleasure. James walked by, anger apparent on his face not even looking at me. I imagined that look in another place in time only he knew it was me and hated me for not being who he thought.

At 1:00 a.m. I was on my way home. The car cruised smoothly down the highway weaving through traffic. Then they came. They fell. I realized for the first time that I'd never be able to be in a committed relationship because I was forced to be at Carl's disposal. How would I explain myself? I couldn't. Once again I sank into my lonely place, then when I arrived home I couldn't sleep so I wrote Sharon a letter. It was filled with things about the move, my upcoming busy schedule, and anything else I could think of that didn't have to do with my night job.

Chapter 21

Diane

I'm in love

The next morning I unpacked the little that I had while waiting for the phone company to arrive. Around 10:00 a.m. a guy showed up and worked on my line for a few minutes then wrote down my new number. Anxious to call James and give it to him like he asked, I sat on the floor and dialed his direct line. Of course he was unavailable but I was transferred to his assistant who took my message and promised James would return my call as soon as possible.

Pleased with her response I hung up with a grin on my face and went out to do some shopping. Several hours and many shopping bags later I returned home exhausted. The first and most important item I pulled from my bag was an answering machine. I wanted to make sure James could always leave a message. There was nothing I could do if he called while I was out but from that moment on I'd always know when he called.

My furniture was scheduled to be delivered the next day so in the meantime I laid a few blankets on the floor in front of my fireplace and settled in for some rest. With my phone by my side I laid there for two hours waiting for James to return my call but he never did. I wondered why he hadn't called. Was he busy with work or was he busy with another woman? I reasoned that I had no business claiming a man as my own after meeting him only once.

It was Wednesday. By Saturday my life was going to be hectic again with rehearsals everyday and other preparations for upcoming shows. I wanted to spend more time with James before all that started. Just after sundown my phone rang loudly at my head startling me to shaking. My excitement to finally speak to James and being jolted from sleep was almost too much for my system to handle.

I answered the call then my excitement waned and my stomach churned. My nerves. My hands were shaking. It was Carl.

"Diane, you were stunning in blue but you didn't get much accomplished last night. You seemed to be preoccupied with something or someone. That's not what I'm looking for. I'm looking for that girl that knows what she wants and does what she has to, to get it. If I had to grade what I saw last night I'd give you a C-. You better get out there and earn your success by helping me. I hold the keys to your future and no one else. Remember that. And just so you know, don't think that just because your schedule is going to be packed that your favors to me end. They'll never end because what I can promise you is unparallel. I have some high paying clients who want private parties. I know what your schedule is like. If I need you outside of that time you better be available or make yourself available – understood?"

"Yes, I understand," I said in a small submissive voice.

"That's what I like. Now don't think that I don't hold poor performance against my girls. I've made the decision to extend my mercy and allow you to continue on without punishment. However, the next time you perform less than what I expect you will be punished, and don't think all my punishments are the same."

"Click."

I dropped the receiver on the floor and held my head in my hands, slowly rocking back and forth. I contemplated suicide but I'd never do that. I wasn't sure what I believed about God but deep down I knew killing myself was wrong. Sitting there a few more moments I picked up the receiver and slowly replaced it. Instantly the phone sounded startling me once again. The call must've come through while I was recovering from Carl's call.

"Hello?" I asked shakily.

"Diane? It's James. What's wrong?"

"Oh nothing's wrong," I said clearing my throat and drying my face with my hands. "How are you?" I asked wanting to know everything he did since meeting him a few days earlier. All the while questions about his presence at Carl's party screamed in my mind.

"Oh I'm doing much better now that I've gotten a chance to speak with you again. There's always a chance that the one you want to, won't call you. I'm glad you did. Yon won't regret it."

"I'm sure I won't," I said through a huge grin. I hoped he couldn't tell I was grinning the way I was.

165

"I'd like to see you."

"When do you want to see me?"

"Right now."

"Alright, we can meet up somewhere in about an hour. Just give me a chance to shower and change real quick. So where do you want to meet?"

"Outside your door in thirty minutes."

"What?"

"I'm on the phone across the street. I meant it when I said I want to see you now."

My heart was racing with anticipation and nervousness. I couldn't wait to see him again, to be near him again. "Okay, I'll hurry so you won't be waiting long." I hung up and ran to the bathroom tripping over bags and shoes.

Smelling good and feeling fresh I opened my door and left. It felt good to be nervous about being with him. I really liked him and it wasn't because of who he was and how much money he had. I genuinely liked him. The doorman opened the door for me and James stepped out of the limo watching my every step. He made me nervous in a good way as I concentrated on not falling in the heels I was wearing. When I reached the car he took my hand in his and kissed the back of it. A wave of goose bumps traveled up my arms and the little girl inside me that liked fairytales wanted to giggle but I suppressed it not wanting to appear silly.

Our first date was one to remember. We had so much fun. We talked about Jersey, our families, our new lives in L.A. and any and everything we could think of. He wined and dined me. There were red roses in the limo, roses at the restaurant, and a huge bouquet of orange tiger lilies and yellow tulips for me during a carriage ride. All of that happened in one night. It was about midnight when we both decided it was time to rap up our night together.

We kissed three times. Once in the carriage, once in the limo, and then at my door. I was definitely without a doubt hooked then. All I could do was think about his soft lips covering mine and our tongues touching and dancing. He turned toward the elevator and I watched him walk away. I heard beautiful music the whole time we were together.

I put my key in the door, turned the knob and pushed. Then as if on cue my other life, the life that threatened to ruin me was inside as loud as ever like a siren. The red button on my answering machine blinked. It seemed to blink with urgency. I took off my heels, unzipped my outfit and headed to my room. After changing I walked by the machine again wishing it could be anyone that left a message for me but truly knowing it could only be Carl because he was the only one that had my number besides James.

"*Beep. Diane, I need you in Brentwood, Beverly Hills, Malibu, Brentwood, Beverly Hills, Malibu…*"

CHAPTER 22

Diane

Bittersweet

A whole year later and nothing had changed much between Carl and I. I was still "on call" no matter how tired I was after shows, appearances, talk shows, or radio shows. By day I was someone famous, a beautiful celebrity who had it all, a beautiful voice, expensive things, a handsome man, but beneath it all just barely beneath the surface and a few hours away I was busy giving myself away for all of it, sometimes two and three nights a week.

I was tired, worn out, and used up and feared I was starting to slip because a few times I found myself about to tell James about Carl but I caught myself. My singing career was doing great because of all the things I went through. I was just beginning my solo career so despite my troubles I was happy that my sacrifice wasn't in vain.

❦

I was packing for a nine month overseas tour and I was excited. James and I were still together. He was the source of all my happiness. I loved him and he loved me. I was due in London the next day to kick off my tour so James and I spent all the time we could together until we could barely keep our eyes open. James was at my place and I asked him to stay and he did. Awakened by a kiss the next morning, James kneeled at my bedside and looked at me.

"Diane I wish I could take you to the airport to see you off but I've been pushing this client off for weeks because of my wanting to spend time with you. Make sure you call me Dee, no matter what time it is here, okay?" he asked kissing me again and again. "Don't forget I'm going to meet you in Japan in a couple months so we'll be able to spend some time together then. Oh, one more thing. I'm proud of you Babe."

"Thank you," I said teary eyed. I sat up and hugged him, then walked him to the door. We kissed and he left.

My public life was going well. I had a wonderful relationship, a blossoming solo singing career, a supportive sister, and amazing fans. It was my hidden life that I wasn't happy with, but what no one knew wouldn't hurt me.

CHAPTER 23

Diane

Dream Interrupted

Arriving in London I exhaled. I hadn't been there since my first tour with Classique. I stepped off the elevator and walked toward the doors of my suite. It was a lovely room, spacious and open, with lots of light. I took five steps inside and all the love I thought I left behind met me. There were vases of roses and vases of tulips placed throughout the main room. I opened the card on the largest bouquet that was placed on a table in front of a window.

To my heart,

I miss you. I'll be seeing you soon.

I love you,

James

"I love you too," I whispered and placed the card in my purse. "I can't wait to see you," I said while enjoying the sweet smell of a rose.

☙

The first month was great. I performed all over England then we packed up and left for Scotland. The third month we traveled to Japan. Things were going great. I was singing like I never have before and had lots of energy because I was feeding off of the energy of my fans. I loved them.

The beginning of the third month James arrived just like we planned. I hated leaving him when I rehearsed for shows, wishing I could be in his arms, but he never complained. Sometimes he sat in the audience watching, claiming he enjoyed seeing me work, watching me shine on stage. He could only stay two weeks, and sadly it seemed like much less time than that, but I was able to schedule two days of rest to make it up to him.

During those two days James and I stayed inside my suite the whole time except to get some fresh air once or twice. Not long after that I found myself embracing him then watching him walk down a terminal to an awaiting plane. I felt lonely again, but one good thing about being overseas and on tour was that Carl didn't bother me. I could actually live my life like a normal person and enjoy my career.

Then one day about a month and a half after James left I was standing during rehearsal and felt a blanket of indescribable tiredness cover me. I shook my head and hands and kicked out my legs trying to shake the sleepiness that had come over me. It was only 5:00 p.m. but my body was telling me otherwise. We still had an hour of rehearsal left but I knew I wasn't going to be able to make it through.

"Guys, I don't know what's wrong with me, but I am beyond beat. I need to leave to get some rest because if I don't I'm gonna fall out right where I stand. I'm serious." A few minutes later I was in a car on my way back to my suite.

"Ms. Frazier, do you need help to the door?" My driver asked.

"No, no. I'm alright Thomas, thank you though. I think I can make it," I said slowly stepping out of the limo one foot at a time. Even though there were less than ten steps to the door I closed my eyes trying to get just a little bit of sleep on the way. My bag slipped from my shoulder. Then moments later it slipped again. In the elevator I weakly pushed the button for my floor and almost poured onto the hall floor once the doors slid open.

Walking into my suite like a zombie I trudged over to the couch one heavy step at a time. Halfway there I realized I may've forgotten to close and lock the door. I turned around slowly hoping it wasn't true but the door was wide open. Whimpering I turned myself around and made the few footstep hike back to the door.

When I finally made it to the couch I fell in a heavy heap onto it. I fell into one of the deepest sleeps I'd ever experienced. I was fully clothed and didn't care. I felt like I was sinking deeper and deeper into the couch. It was a lovely sleep. As I sank in I wondered what was wrong with me then

I didn't care as my mouth opened and my arm fell off the couch causing my hand to lay limply on the plush carpet.

I awoke five hours later around ten thirty. It was terribly dark all around me. I slowly sat up and wiped drool from my cheek and the corner of my mouth. I was still beyond tired but the five hour nap I took gave me enough energy to get to my room and change. I fell into the bed beneath the covers and slept. My 8:00 a.m. alarm went off but I didn't hear it as I dreamt of my parents and sister.

Sharon was trying to tell me something and my parents were standing off to the side. My mom looked like she was crying into her hands. Her face was covered with her hands and her shoulders shook. My dad was trying to console her. We were all in the same room and my parents stood several feet behind Sharon to the right and Sharon stood in front of me several feet away. She and I were both looking at our parents but I was standing behind her, a little further away from them than she was. Then she turned and faced me when my dad looked up with pleading in his eyes. His left arm was around mom's shoulders and his right hand moved in a pleading gesture. Sharon's face looked alarmed and her eyes were big. She opened her mouth to say something to me but she was ringing, I mean the phone was ringing and I was snatched from my dream.

I sat up and turned the alarm clock around. It was blaring and the phone was screaming. I didn't know which to address first. I quickly decided to answer the phone so whoever it was wouldn't hang up then I violently turned the alarm clock off knocking it to the floor.

"Hello?" I asked.

"Diane, where are you?" my choreographer asked.

"Oh shoot!" I said, "I'm sorry, I overslept. I'm getting up right now."

"Don't worry about it. It's 10:00 a.m. now, and we need at least four hours to go over the steps to get the routine right. During the last show I noticed you and a back up dancer mis-stepped. It hurt me to see it. I'm not going to create something especially for you and you get on stage and do it however you want. I need dedication from you."

"I know, I'm sorry. When is the next rehearsal?"

"Let me see," she said flipping through pages. "Since you blew this one I can meet you around one."

"Unh, unh," I said going through my schedule in my mind. "Sorry one is no good because I'm giving a radio interview."

"Okay listen, if you can get Darren over to your suite then I'll come

172

there and work with you guys after hours. I want everything too look pretty up there."

"Thanks, so much Felecia."

"You're welcome. See you later."

I knew I had to get myself together so I got out of bed feeling way better than I did before getting into it and headed to the bathroom for a shower. I ordered room service afterward and read the L.A. Times I requested as I waited. I ordered grits, scrambled eggs, sausage, toast, and orange juice. Everything smelled so good when it was brought in but when the lid was removed from the plate there was something about the eggs. I couldn't stand the sight nor the smell of them. My appetite pulled back a little.

I began taking a new type of vitamin about a week or two before and I noticed that I felt a little nauseous after taking it if I ate light, so despite the eggs I ate everything on my plate, drank almost the entire pitcher of orange juice, then feeling full took my vitamin. Around 1:00 p.m. I felt nauseous. Just before the interview I felt it.

"What on earth is wrong with me?" I asked myself. The interview lasted about an hour and I couldn't wait until it was over so I could get something to eat. I figured the vitamins were too potent or just didn't agree with my system so I threw them away. I had a huge lunch hoping to get rid of the nausea but although it helped I still felt a sick feeling in the center of my chest that threatened to rise up my throat.

"I've got to make a doctor's appointment," I said out loud to no one in particular. Other patrons of the restaurant turned to look at me when I spoke out loud because I was eating alone. When I got back to my suite I called my doctor and he told me he'd be right over. Thank God he was in the same hotel but on a different floor. When he got there he asked me all the basic questions and I answered them. I never knew what he was thinking until he said it because he hardly ever showed any expression. When he finished examining me he asked to see the vitamins and I showed them to him.

"Diane is there any chance you could be pregnant?"

"What?" I asked.

"Pregnant," he repeated.

"Pregnant?"

"Yes, pregnant. Have you been taking the birth control pills I prescribed for you?"

"Yes."

"Have you been taking them everyday?"

"Yes."

"Well, in that case you must remember there's a very small chance of a woman becoming pregnant while on the pill. Are you sure you've been taking them?"

At that moment I remembered that I'd been so busy thinking about my freedom from Carl while on tour that I didn't bring any birth control with me at all! I was so caught up with rehearsing and the tour and then with James when he visited that I really hadn't taken the time to sit down and think.

"Actually doctor, I haven't taken any pills for the past few months. Now that we're on the subject I haven't had a period for about two months but I thought it was stress and would work itself out. I just didn't realize, didn't think," I said starting to cry. My face was in my hands and tears were seeping through my fingers.

"Take it easy Diane. Just breathe."

I was really getting out of control so he helped me to my bedroom. "Diane that was just a diagnosis based on the facts you gave me. I'll need a urine sample and some blood from you to be absolutely sure."

"So there's still a chance that I may not be pregnant?" I asked sounding pitiful.

"Diane, I'm not going to lie to you. I think you're pregnant. Let me get everything I need in the other room and we can get these tests run."

I sat and waited. About an hour later there was a knock at my door. I checked the peephole and saw my doctor standing there looking serious as usual.

"Well, I have the results," he said killing me with suspense. "You're absolutely pregnant. I need to examine you and check your cervix to estimate how far along you are. I'll give you a call with a location in about fifteen minutes. I assume you're going to keep the baby so I took the liberty of filling a prenatal vitamin prescription for you. Throw those other things back in the trash." He stopped and looked at me and for the first time he showed some emotion. "I know this pregnancy was unplanned but it's not the end of the world. I brought you the prenatal vitamins hoping and if need be to plead with you not to abort the baby. Being a celebrity physician I've documented countless abortions, an innumerable and appalling count of aborted babies all in the name of image, a career, and lifestyle."

I'd never taken the time to seriously consider children because my career and now James were all I ever thought about. Now I was faced with a pregnancy and I didn't know what to do about it.

"I appreciate your concern," I told my doctor. "Thank you for everything." I shut the door behind him and slid down it with my back to it and cried and cried and cried. *How could you be so stupid? How could you forget about the pills? Okay, okay. Get yourself together Diane. You can do it. Just get yourself together so you can clear your head and think,"* I said out loud to myself. *"Okay, what's next, what's next. Oh! I have to call Darren. Once he's here I'll call Felecia then we can work on the dance steps."*

I tried pushing the reality of my pregnancy out of my mind. I decided that the more I didn't think about it the less it could affect me. Of course I was wrong. The next thing I knew my phone rang. It was my doctor calling. He said he could examine me within the next thirty minutes if I had the time. I thought about it. Curiosity made me agree and I jotted down the address.

Once I hung up with him I contacted Darren to see if he could rehearse in my room, but I didn't' get an answer. I called Felecia to let her know and she sucked her teeth in exasperation but we agreed that Darren and I would stay late after the next rehearsal to get the moves right.

I stood up to get my jacket and my hand immediately went to my stomach. *"Diane stop it,"* I said to myself. During the exam my doctor confirmed that I was about eight to nine weeks pregnant. He gave me some information to read on what things to expect like the changes my body would go through as well as do's and don'ts and how to eat healthy despite not wanting to.

I knew James was the father but deep down inside I had a fear that one of Carl's guests could be the father. I knew it wasn't true because during those times I took my pill daily. But I still thought about it. I considered calling James to tell him but I didn't know how to say it. I thought about waiting to tell him after I got home but I figured he'd have a problem with it, plus there were a few more months left of the tour.

My doctor gave me an estimated due date of March 20, 1978. I knew my career was over, because the success of my career depended on my performance for Carl. He wasn't going to want anything to do with a pregnant woman entertaining his guests. Though the thought crossed my mind that some men would, and then I quickly shoved the thought away.

I knew I was in trouble. Day by day the morning sickness I experienced became worse. I had no idea why it was called morning sickness and not

175

just sick because I felt sick throughout the day and into the evening. I tried to overpower the sickness by eating salty things like corn chips, sunflower seeds, and pretzels. They all helped a little but nothing could defeat the sick feeling. In the mornings, the sickness began as soon as my feet hit the floor. I must say I was quite miserable.

Not only that, I was beginning to feel quite uncomfortable in my clothes and I was nervous. I was nervous and scared because I was on tour promoting my first solo album overseas and I was pregnant for the first time and couldn't tell anyone. I didn't want anyone to know, but with a few months left of the tour, everyone would soon find out because both my appearance and performance were changing. I was a wreck and needed to come up with a plan.

Lying in bed one morning with a trashcan on my lap, ready to catch anything, I decided I couldn't take it. I couldn't finish the tour because I felt miserable and was looking the part too. I was putting on a little weight because I was stuffing myself with foods to keep the morning sickness at bay, plus it didn't help that my appetite had grown in the process. I was no longer the lean and sexy siren all the magazines and entertainment reporters described me as. I was a mess and all I wanted to do was sleep and eat and do it in peace.

I decided that the tour had to end. All my upcoming shows, all the tickets purchased, and all my adoring fans had to go. I was upset to say the least but what could I do? I had to make several phone calls. Calls to my people to get the tour wrapped up, a call to Sharon to explain what's going on so she wouldn't be worried when the media broadcasted the story, and finally to James, but not necessarily in that order.

I decided to call James last, I called my sister first, then I called all the people in my camp that needed to know what was going on so they could decide what story they'd tell the press. Sharon was concerned, surprised, happy, and then concerned again. Everyone on tour was simply told that I had fallen ill and couldn't complete the tour. I got a lot of sympathy because they knew how important the whole tour was to me and for me.

The others on tour with me had mixed feelings. They were sad for me but at the same time hurt that they too had to return home. I ruined a lot of plans and dreams, and that weighed on me. When I picked up the phone to call James I became uncontrollably nervous and had to hang the receiver back up. My hands were sweating and shaking. I had to remind myself that James knew nothing of my secret and that he'd be happy that I was pregnant – I guessed. He said he wanted children one day. I said the same thing too but not at twenty years old, because I surely wasn't ready.

I needed to hear James' voice. I needed to hear him tell me that he loved me and that he'd take care of me and that everything would be alright like he'd been doing the past year. I needed to know that I wasn't alone. Drying my sweaty hands on the blanket pulled up around my waist I slowly dialed James' home number.

It was 9:00 a.m. Friday in Sydney where I was so I guessed it to be sometime Thursday afternoon in Los Angeles. The line was ringing. After I counted six rings I began to wonder where he was. On the eighth ring he picked up.

"Hello?"

"Hey Baby," I said mustering up a cheery voice.

"Hey Babe. We agreed we'd take turns calling each other. You called me last and I don't want your bill getting high. With you in Australia who knows how much this call will be," he said laughing knowing darn well neither one of us was worried about a phone bill.

"I know but I miss you, plus I have something important to talk to you about." It was quiet on his end. I knew his brain was working overtime because my tone of voice left no hint as to what I wanted to discuss. I heard him exhale.

"Okay, what about?" I heard something in his voice. I couldn't pinpoint whether it was fear, dread or what. I didn't want to prolong things and beat around the bush so I just came out with it.

"James, I'm about two months pregnant."

More silence.

"Are you serious?" My heart pounded fiercely now in my chest.

"Yes. I've been feeling sick and tired and even sicker so I called my doctor and he ran some tests. The tests prove I'm pregnant and his exam showed I'm about eight to nine weeks along. Plus I haven't had a period since before you visited me in Japan.

"Wow," was all I heard. "I can't believe this."

I couldn't tell what emotion he was feeling and the suspense was too much for me.

"I gotta come see you," he said with a smile in his voice. "Man, I'm gonna be a dad! This is great! I'm gonna make arrangements to fly out in the morning. I..."

"Wait," I said, "I've decided to end the tour and I'll probably be leaving

Sydney in a few days I guess. Why waste the money on plane fare when I'll be home soon?"

"Because I want to see you and my baby as soon as I can," he said.

"Okay," I said wanting to see him too. "Call me when you've landed and I'll pick you up."

"You sound like you're about to hang up."

"I am. I'm so tired babe. You just don't know how being pregnant drains your energy," I said almost nodding off in the comfort of the conversation we were having.

"Alright, I'll let you guys rest. I love you."

"I love you too. Be careful."

"I will. Bye."

"Bye," I said softly as I fell into a peaceful sleep with my mind and heart at ease.

❧

Grinning from ear to ear, James considered his upcoming role as a father. He liked the idea of it. After the joy of the surprise settled in his heart he felt the guilt again. *Diane and I created a life outside the walls of marriage. I knew better than that just like I knew better than to mess around with Francine. I don't want my child in this world a single day with parents that are not married. But am I ready to get married? Am I ready to marry Diane? I once told Francine that I was waiting for God to send the right woman at the right time. I wonder if she remembers that? Diane can't possibly be the one. Look at the life she lives! Man, look at the life I'm living!*

CHAPTER 24

Diane

No more secrets?

When I received James' call I quickly dressed and called my driver. We drove to the airport and waited about fifteen minutes before I finally spotted James. Once he got inside the car I looked at him deeply holding his face in my hands. I decided I could love him forever.

We ended up staying in Sydney a week longer and flew back home that Saturday. James wanted to wait on me all day long and I wasn't about to say no as ill as I was feeling. I felt bad that I wasn't much company most of the time because I slept, but he said he enjoyed watching me sleep with his hand on my stomach. Those days were so good, so warm, so wonderful to fall asleep in his arms knowing I was loved.

I loved being taken care of by the man I loved. James and I agreed that I'd stay at his place until the baby was born. We didn't make plans beyond that because thinking about the baby consumed us. However, I overheard James on the phone one day speaking with someone about purchasing some land and something about new construction. I was pretty sure he wanted to surprise me with a beautiful home when I returned home after having the baby. I smiled thinking about how wonderful he was.

During the day when James was at the office I slept and ate and did maternity exercises that my doctor suggested. I didn't want to snoop around because I knew James trusted me, so I didn't the first two weeks. The third week I couldn't stand it any longer so I looked through his bedroom. I was surprised to not find anything. Friends told me about how men don't think anything about things like pictures of old girlfriends, their numbers or different articles of clothing and may leave them thrown about because what's the past is the past.

With me I'd throw that number, the love letters and cards, and pictures out as soon as possible. I found none of those things. I even checked his closet, his dresser drawers, inside shoe boxes, hat boxes, and coat and jacket pockets. I checked under the mattress, in his nightstands, between pages of books in his library, and even between the pages of his Bible. Damp with perspiration and out of breathe because of the extra weight I was carrying, I stopped my inspection and gave James an A+.

I totally trusted him and he trusted me and everything in my world was good until one day just before James was due home, I turned the television to the news and at the same time the phone rang. The media had been broadcasting news about my cancelled tour since the week I returned home. They said more information would soon follow.

I didn't know whether my publicist would release the fact that I'd become pregnant because everyone knew I wasn't married, but he advised me that a statement would be made soon because my fans needed to know and many were unhappy that the tour ended early without much of an explanation.

I trusted my publicist so I knew the right statement would be made for me and my fans. I decided I wouldn't worry myself about it. Besides, the media seemed to be satisfied that I caught the flu.

After turning the television down I answered the phone and my little cocoon of safety and bliss immediately crumbled and blew away. It was Carl.

"I hope you've enjoyed your little break. What? Didn't you think I'd contact you sooner or later? Remember, you belong to me. This has happened before to one of my girls but I hear Mr. James Anderson is the father. You two look so happy when you're out together like you have no care in the world. That's all about to change unless you get rid of that baby and get yourself together to get back on tour in a few months and get back to paying me back. Remember, nothing in life is free Diane and you owe me. That nice condo you have belongs to me because you paid for it with money you earned by working for me. You're not about to change your role and try to become wife and mommy of the year and think you can back out of our little contract you signed. You better make up your mind what you're going to do Diane, and just in case you need a little help making the right decision I've sent you a little something at home and to Mr. Anderson's residence. Its proof that I'm running things, you belong to me, and that I won't be crossed."

"Click." He hung up on me then I heard James' key in the door.

As he was opening the door a delivery man who I recognized as an employee of Carl's handed James a package! I almost jumped out of my skin when I realized who he was and saw the dimensions of the package he carried.

"Oh God, no!" I said out loud as I hurried to the door to take the package from James. He looked at me like I was crazy then thanked the guy and shut and locked the door after giving him a tip. "How was your day honey?" I asked not even trying to hide the fact that I was out of breath.

"First you need to sit down. I don't want to see you running around like that. You weren't paying attention to where you were going and almost bumped into the coffee table. I hope you're more careful than that during the day."

"Of course. Of course I am. I was just excited to get this delivery. I ordered it a little while ago and it's just getting here. I thought I was going to have to call the company to find out what was going on."

"Oh yeah? Well, what it is that has you so excited?" He asked giving me his full attention. I really wished he'd just go to the bedroom to shower and change like he always did but for some reason he sat down on the couch motioning for me to come to him.

"Uh, ummm..." I stammered. Just then the phone rang again and I lunged to answer it but James beat me to it and caught me before I fell face first onto one of the chairs surrounding the coffee table.

"Hello?" He said with a question in his voice. He had an expression on his face that asked, "Who in the world is calling right now when I'm trying to figure out why the woman carrying my baby is going crazy. "Oh, hi Denise. No, that's alright. I know you wouldn't have called if it wasn't important. Wow, I forgot to sign those documents. Yes, I'd rather you go ahead and sign my name, but I really didn't get a good look at them. I'm coming back to the office to review the package and sign everything so it can be mailed this evening. Okay, see you in about twenty minutes."

By that time James had already let me go and I'd walked off to the bedroom getting into bed, pulling the covers over myself to feign tiredness, thinking I'd get off the hook.

"Uh-oh," I said when I heard his footsteps getting closer to the bedroom. I scooted further under the covers and couldn't decide whether to have my eyes opened or closed. I decided to leave them open.

"Diane are you alright?!" He asked with alarm in his voice, then sat down next to me.

Quick. Think, think. "No, I feel a little dizzy. I think I turned around too fast to answer the phone. Thank God you caught me before I fell onto the chair."

"Diane, it looked more like you tried to attack the phone than losing your balance. You know the doctor said the first trimester is when most miscarriages happen. You know what? I'm calling an agency to have a nurse here at all times. I want to make sure you and the baby are safe."

"James I'm just about four months in, so we're past that point. I'm okay- really. We're fine and I don't need a nurse sitting around watching my every move."

"I understand, but I'd never forgive myself if anything happened to the two of you and there was something I could've done to prevent it. Please."

He held my hands in his and I couldn't say no. "Okay."

"Good. I'm calling an agency in the morning to have someone sent over as soon as possible. I'm leaving for the office now and should be back in an hour or two. I'd like to eat dinner with you but if you get too hungry before I get back go ahead and order take out and I'll eat when I get back." He kissed me and left.

When I heard the door shut and lock I picked up the phone to call a car. I stuffed the package in my purse and waited ten minutes before leaving. The driver waited beside the car and opened and closed my door for me. "I need to go to my place," I said and we were off. I only had an hour or so to do what I wanted to do. I planned to get the package, see what it was and get rid of it.

❧

When I stepped around the corner after leaving the elevator, I peered down the hall and saw the package on the floor in front of my door. I hurried as quickly as I could and grabbed it. Once I stepped inside my condo I almost had a heart attack.

As if it were wallpaper, there were huge, nude poster-sized pictures of me and different men all over my living room wall! Each man's face was blurred, but mine shone brightly as if I was the only one accountable for the things we did. I ran and started ripping the posters down one by one. One after the other I ripped paper off the walls until I created a huge heap in the middle of the floor. I was sweating and a couple of my fingers were bleeding and pounding with pain because a few times I dug into the wall and broke fingernails. I hurried to the kitchen ignoring the pain in my belly and grabbed a box of trash bags. It must've taken me an hour to

182

rip everything down and clean up. Afterward I leaned over the kitchen counter to rest and catch my breath. Then I reached down and massaged my stomach as my breathing slowed.

I poured myself a glass of water and headed to the answering machine. One after the other I listened to and erased messages from Carl, Sharon, Carl, Sharon, then Carl, Carl, Carl. I let the last message from Carl play as I unbuttoned my pants standing before my toilet to sneek a peek at the crotch of my panties. Deep down I secretly wished I'd see blood but there was none. Then my last bit of hope died because my heart wasn't hard enough to get an abortion. I loved James but I did not want to have his baby. When I got right down to the nitty gritty of this whole situation, my career was what mattered most.

Snatched away from my secret thoughts I returned my attention to Carl's messages as a new one began. It was a particularly nasty message where he demeaned me, James, and the fetus I was carrying. The message after that happened to be from Carla. She didn't hold anything back either. I rewound it just so I could be absolutely sure that it was actually her. I couldn't believe she could be so evil. I listened quietly in disbelief as the real Carla revealed herself.

"Hi Diane. I haven't heard from you in a while. Not since you were throwing a tantrum about the contract you signed. No one forced you to sign it. You signed it on your own because you're a stupid little girl that ran away from home to get away from mommy and daddy because they didn't believe in you," she said in a sing song voice. "Yeah, I like your place. I think I'll enjoy throwing parties there when Carl buys the building and kicks you out on the street for trying to burn him. Yeah I can see that. Oh, I just had to tell you that the blue get up you had on at Carl's lounge was "boss", but I think I had more heads turning, especially a special someone that's close to you. I wonder what he was doing there with me? I saw you watching thinking I didn't realize who you were with your little blue wig on and that mask. I knew it was you. I guess if you were woman enough he wouldn't have felt the need to spend time in the company of other women. And not only are you stupid, but you're irresponsible. You went and got yourself knocked up. But I have to hand it to you for convincing your man that it's his."

Then she laughed and laughed and laughed. I just stood there and yelled, "It is his! It is his!" I grabbed the laughing answering machine and threw it to the floor. I stomped it wishing it was Carla's face and screamed out, "I hate you! I hate you! I hate you!" In agony fell to my knees then gently onto my spreading backside and cried like a baby.

A few moments later I raised my head to get up because I realized I had to head back to James' place. When I stood up completely all time ceased because James was standing in the doorway staring at me in disbelief. He had an expression on his face that I'd only seen in my dreams. I awakened from those dreams glistening with sweat and panting for breath because they seemed so real. I feared James finding out somehow, but I never thought it would be like this. Finally, my fears became reality and my secret was out. James knew I was a whore and I had nothing to say. The only comfort I had in life stood before me hurt and speechless yet the right words escaped me.

Ashamed, I broke his gaze and he turned and left in a hurry, I supposed out of my life forever, leaving me to raise a baby on my own or maybe not. I stood there trembling, face wet with tears, and nose running carefree. I walked to the door that I forgot to close because of the shock of seeing my secret life splashed across the room. I locked it like I should have in the first place then sat down on my loveseat that silently pointed its finger at me and laughed.

It laughed because I sat upon it alone except for the child I carried in my womb that was causing me so much trouble and grief. Explanations as to why James showed up surfaced through my clouded thoughts and I remembered that he'd forgotten the day before to pick up some things for me. Trustworthy James was making good on his promise to remember to stop by my place.

CHAPTER 25

Diane

I think I get it now...

My blurry eyes focused and scanned the room. I'd done a pretty good job of ripping the posters down and I almost got away with it. *Almost got away with it.* James didn't deserve to be with a stupid, lying tramp like me anyway.

On the opposite wall hung a picture that reminded me of one of my favorite things about growing up in New Jersey. It captured an autumn day, maybe from the past or sometime in the future. Trees were adorned with red, orange, brown, and amber leaves. The talented artist expertly depicted golden sunlight cascading through the tree tops and ever so often there was a leaf that fell from its place on its tree.

After gazing at the picture for a number of minutes my eyes saw those trees swaying back and forth and they spoke to each other about each leaf that somehow represented an aspect of life that would occur at its appointed time. I closed my eyes and envisioned myself a tree there swaying and cooled by the fall breeze and warmed by the autumn sun. One by one, then two by two, then one more I lost a leaf to the winds of life wishing I could pick up and hold onto some. The others I wished had never belonged to me.

As the tree, I peered up at the sky waving my limbs in gratitude and praise knowing my Creator was high above me watching every moment and providing my every need. I the tree testified of God's goodness and faithfulness to me for providing the rain when I was thirsty and the sun when I needed nutrients. The beauty of my existence told the world that God indeed exists.

Now I sat in my living room pitying myself with regrets. I looked back at the picture and knew that the silent story the trees told should be my own except even greater. There was no way I could deny God's constant intervention in my life. He spoke to me through family, strangers, and situations but I chose to ignore Him, chose to call Him a lie. At the lowest point in my life, I was carrying a child that was not welcome and would probably never be welcome because of all that transpired surrounding the child's conception. What if I lost the man I love? I was enslaved because of the very thing I ran to L.A. to do. It was then that I knew that no one could help me but the very One I denied each time I made the wrong decision. Yet in the tenderness of my disgrace I felt a place in my battered heart open.

Dear God. Please help me.

Falling Leaves

Leaves fall slowly from the tree of my life.

These leaves are the colors of fall because

they are falling to the ground.

I do not know which leaf will touch the

ground first.

It seems that just before a leaf is to skim a

blade of grass, the wind blows and the

leaves of my life begin to fall in different

orders again.

When the leaves of my life do touch the

ground it does not matter where on the

ground they fall.

For they will all arise in spring even

more beautiful than when they fell

from my tree of life.

QUESTIONS AND TOPICS

FOR DISCUSSION

1. Which character in the story do you identify with most? Why?

2. How did pride cause James to eventually stumble and fall?

3. How did pride affect the course of Diane's life?

4. Discuss the role of temptation in the book. How do Diane and James deal with temptation in their respective relationships?

5. Marlene clearly tells Diane that Carla is not to be trusted. Have you ever been in a situation where someone told you not to trust someone, yet you did and the situation turned out bad? What happened?

6. "You guys never became anything more than what you started out as but you had dreams. What happened?... You two are just two old scared black people that don't have nothin', don't want nothin', and ain't never gonna have nothin' because you're scared of failing!" (Chap.1)

Although Diane was disrespectful when she made this statement to her parents, do you agree with what she said? Do you agree that sometimes we or others can become afraid to step out on faith? Discuss.

7. "I was going through something on that seat but didn't know what... Although the walk to the end of the prayer line wasn't long it seemed like a mile... in my mind I kept hearing something say "get in line, go get in line" and I kept thinking "no, no, no". (Chap. 2)

James' mental battle prior to accepting Jesus as his Savior is one that many Christians can relate to. If you are saved discuss your experience just before accepting Christ. If you're not saved have you ever experienced what James experienced but decided to wait until another time to accept Jesus? If so, why? Do you feel differently now? Discuss.

8. As they passed my window I heard Carla say between clenched teeth, "I told you never to come here no matter what!"...Okay, so Carla had something going on and I wondered what it was. I didn't think too much of it though because Carla and I were still getting to know each other. That girl could've been one of her acting friends from work... I decided to ask Carla about it later...maybe. (Chap. 4)

Carla's behavior was suspect the night her visitor came over and Carla promptly escorted her away. Diane decided not to question Carla about it. If you were Diane would you have said something to Carla? Why or why not? Do you believe Carla's actions were odd enough for Diane to consider Marlene's warning about Carla?

9. Then I felt that familiar place in me open up and deep down I knew I needed to get better control of my flesh. I was well aware of my weakness for women but it was something I rarely mentioned in my prayers. (Chap. 5)

In this excerpt James admitted that he had a weakness for women but he rarely addressed it in his prayers. Have you ever experienced a battle to overcome a certain sin but realized you were the problem? Discuss.

Are you currently dealing with a sin(s) that you'd like to stop committing but you are struggling to do so? Take a moment to reflect. Be totally honest about the sin. If you are committed to winning the battle over that sin(s), go quietly before God and admit it. Ask God to help you overcome it. End your prayer in Jesus' name and thank God for doing exactly what you asked.

10. How do you feel about the ending of the book?

Contact Information

Vondalyn encourages readers to visit her online at
www.vondalynshaw.com

For book signings please contact Vondalyn at
vondalynshaw.author@gmail.com